Graphic Designers Surveyed

Graphic Designers Surveyed
a GraphicDesign& Social Science title

[WFG& K]

GraphicDesign& is a pioneering publishing house dedicated to creating intelligent, vivid books that explore how graphic design connects with all other things and the value that it brings.

Established by Lucienne Roberts and Rebecca Wright, GraphicDesign& partners graphic designers with experts from other fields to inform, educate, entertain and provoke – and to challenge perceptions about what and who graphic design is for.

www.graphicdesignand.com

GraphicDesign&

Graphic Designers Surveyed

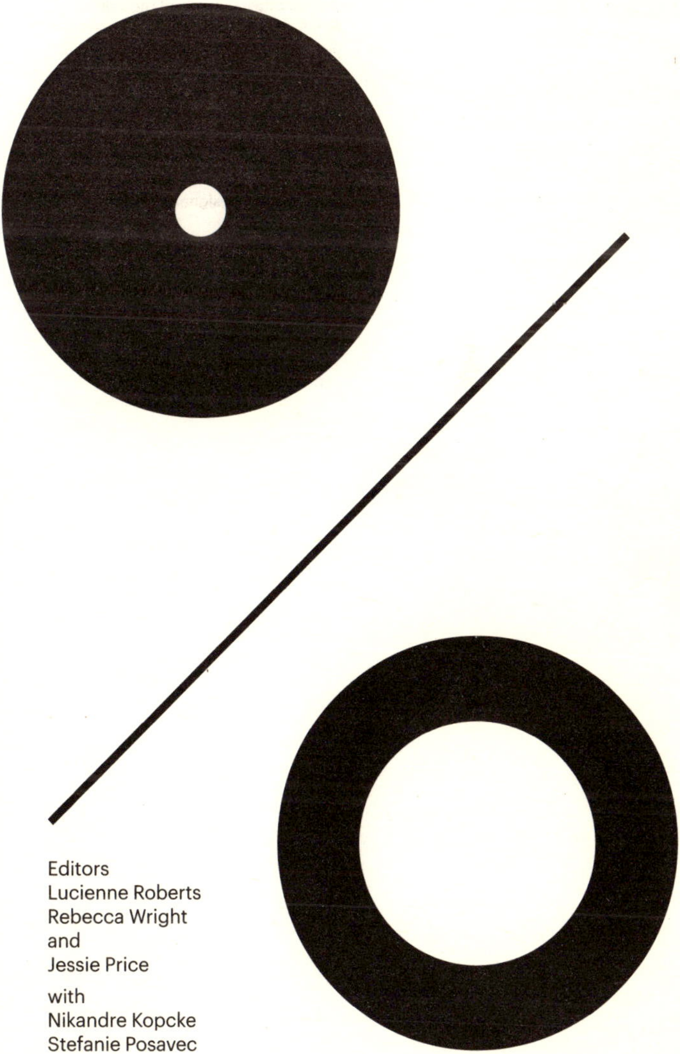

Editors
Lucienne Roberts
Rebecca Wright
and
Jessie Price

with
Nikandre Kopcke
Stefanie Posavec

A GraphicDesign& book

First published in 2015 by
GraphicDesign&
167 Foundling Court
The Brunswick Centre
London WC1N 1AN
UK

+44 [0]20 7490 8880
info@graphicdesignand.com
www.graphicdesignand.com

ISBN 978 0 9572381 2 1

Designed by
LucienneRoberts+

Printed and bound by
CPI Group [UK] Ltd
Croydon, CRO 4YY

Distributed by
Central Books

10 9 8 7 6 5 4 3 2 1

A CIP catalogue record for this book is available from the British Library. While every effort has been made to ensure all factual information contained in this book is correct, in some cases the data and calculations are open to interpretation. All reasonable attempts have been made to trace the copyright holders of images reproduced in this book. If any attribution has been omitted, the publisher will endeavour to amend in any subsequent editions.

Introduction

This section is made up of introductory texts from publishers GraphicDesign& [Lucienne Roberts / Rebecca Wright and Jessie Price] and collaborators Nikandre Kopcke [social scientist] and Stefanie Posavec [data designer]. These are followed by a short explanation of how the data visualisations work throughout the book.

Introduction

Lucienne Roberts / Rebecca Wright
and Jessie Price

Independent publishing house GraphicDesign& [GD&] was set up to explore how graphic design connects with, and brings value to, other subjects.

Our first book, *Page 1: Great Expectations,* was a GD& Literature title. Our second, *Golden Meaning*, was a GD& Mathematics book. In both, the focus was on what graphic design brings to another subject. For our third publication, we decided to turn this relationship around. The focus of *Graphic Designers Surveyed* is us – graphic designers – but seen through the lens of social science.

There are countless books that showcase graphic design itself, but we wanted to know about the people behind the work – who we are and what we do – so we approached social scientist Nikandre Kopcke to help us find out. Having identified what questions we wanted to ask, Nikandre suggested that a survey would be the best way to collect this information... and so began the months [well, years] of survey writing and data gathering that have culminated in this book.

Nikandre set out the questions that any good social scientist would ask about age, gender, income and financial security while, under her watchful eye, we added questions specific to our field – and others that were frankly just a bit nosy. She advised that surveying two comparator populations would be most revealing so we chose to survey the UK and US for their scale and internationally diverse design communities.

Our conversations resulted in the addition of even more targeted questions. Nikandre pointed out those that were leading or where our wording was problematic. She warned us against open answers [see p314 for what happens when you ignore your resident social scientist] and putting words into people's mouths. As the process continued, we discovered some of our own subconscious biases and tried our best to keep these from influencing the final survey.

The survey went live on 25 February 2015 and ran for two months [until 26 April]. We promoted it mainly online: it was featured on both UK- and US-based design-orientated websites. We emailed design agencies and personal contacts asking them to help us spread the word, and we tweeted about it. Respondents were self-selecting – we didn't track down designers who might not find the survey online. Having aimed for around 1,000 responses, we are delighted to have ended up with nearly double that.

Nikandre's initial observation of the results was that 'designers are clearly not used to being surveyed!' She found it charming but slightly odd that people from outside the UK / US had diligently filled out the whole survey despite their data being ineligible for analysis. Respondents also found plenty of space for idiosyncrasy – answers to the question about age included the person who just said 'old', the very precise 31.5-year-old, and the slightly sinister 'you know how old I am'...

From her social science viewpoint, Nikandre found the differences between the UK / US and female / male respondents among the most meaningful – find her observations on p056 and p102.

Applying Nikandre's social science methodology helped us consider new ways of exploring and representing the data. We discovered that mapping one data set on to another gave us some of the most interesting insight. Nikandre was quick to remind us that despite the semblance of objectivity of much data visualisation, graphic design skews all data – how information is presented changes how it is read. Of course graphic design can help increase understanding, which is why our data visualisations are mostly very simple, but we also wanted to showcase the effects of graphic design so invited data designer Stefanie Posavec to bring a more experimental approach to the presentation of some key data. Her contributions demonstrate both the playfulness and subtlety that can be achieved when graphic design and social science meet.

With so many choices to make at every stage of this project, there will be questions that readers wish we had asked, types of graphic designers we didn't reach, or things that we didn't quite manage to capture in our data [we already have our own list of things we missed out]. One of the many things we learned in conducting this survey with the help of a social scientist is that *everything* affects your data, but it is impossible to know exactly how. Did promoting online skew the age range of our designers to be younger – or is that a lazy assumption? Are the women in our sample group younger because women leave the profession earlier, because more young women are coming into the industry, or is it too small a difference to mean anything?

Lucienne Roberts is co-founder of GraphicDesign& and a graphic designer and design writer. The work of her London-based studio LucienneRoberts+ is defined by her intention to make accessible, engaging graphic design with a socially aware agenda. She is a signatory of the *First Things First* 2000 manifesto and a member of the Alliance Graphique Internationale.

Rebecca Wright is co-founder of GraphicDesign& and programme director of Graphic Communication Design at Central Saint Martins, University of the Arts London. As a design educator and writer she has lectured, spoken at events and acted as consultant for academic institutions in the UK and abroad.

Throughout the book, we've tried to avoid drawing conclusions that aren't in the data. Instead, we've stated what's there and asked some of the questions that occurred to us. Having said that, there are some unavoidable observations we would like to share. Among them are that we are variously witty, sarcastic, enthusiastic, frustrated, overworked and yet optimistic. Graphic designers love graphic design but feel misunderstood and undervalued [not something unusual or specific to graphic designers, as Nikandre was quick to point out].

Ultimately, we hope that *Graphic Designers Surveyed* provides insight into who this self-selecting sample of graphic designers are, what they do and how they feel about the profession. While it may not be exhaustive or conclusive, it's a start.

Jessie Price is an associate of GraphicDesign& and a graphic designer working primarily in publishing and the arts. She is currently art director at publisher Head of Zeus and has worked as a researcher and associate lecturer at University of the Arts London. In 2015 she co-wrote *Communication Design: Insights from the Creative Industries*.

Introduction

Nikandre Kopcke, social scientist

There's a great podcast about design called 99% Invisible, and if you're a graphic designer reading this, you probably understand why it's called that. Graphic design is everywhere, and yet it's also almost entirely invisible. Now that screens mediate so much of our communication, design shapes virtually everything we say; more importantly, it shapes the impact of what we say. Design powers the global economy, silently advising us on hundreds of everyday decisions that have nothing to do with design.

It colours how we feel about politicians, counsels us on the reliability of caterers, keeps us loyal to one brand of toothpaste over another, and – come on, let's be honest – tells us what wine to buy for dinner. [Just me?]

And yet, graphic design is something we non-designers rarely notice. In fact, when we do notice design, it tends to be because something's gone wrong. Effective design is invisible; it amplifies the message but doesn't interfere with it. As you might expect, then, the designers who work their black magic on the global economy are also largely unknown to us.

But what's interesting is that they are also largely unknown to themselves; few studies have looked at graphic design as an industry, and there is very little concrete data about who designers are and how they live and work.

I am not a graphic designer – not even close – but invisibility is something I relate to. I was trained as a sociologist; my background is in gender and development and feminist economics. Design and sociology are in most senses polar opposites, and yet in an important sense very similar. Like design, sociology deals in the invisible: the complex social forces that we can't see but that indelibly shape our lives. Unlike design, the job of a sociologist is to make those invisible forces visible. Sociology is all about interfering with the message.

When Lucienne and Rebecca approached me about a GD& collaboration, I knew what I wanted to find out. What if design were the message? What if we dragged graphic designers out of the shadows and asked them prying questions about their lives, their work and what it's like to be a designer in 2015? What if we tried to make all that invisible stuff visible?

Having asked those questions, I can tell you a few things right off the bat. Designers are a nightmare to survey. They frequently disregard instructions and give answers that can best be described, fittingly, as creative [see p446 for some of the best]. Male designers tend to be both creative and grouchy. And almost everyone has a bone to pick with clients.

Hats off to the dedicated contingent of non-US / UK-based designers who ploughed through the entire survey despite being told that they were ineligible to participate. You taught me that social scientists are an oddly rule-abiding group, and I hope that your commitment inspires other comparative surveys.

Finally, a note on interpretation. This book tells us about the group of people we surveyed, but for the most part the results shown don't tell us why things are the way they are. That requires a different kind of analysis, beyond the scope of this research.

It's important to remember this because our instinct is to interpret figures based on our existing knowledge as well as our subjective understanding of the world. We also cannot extrapolate from the results of this survey to the whole graphic design industry – the only people it can tell us about with any certainty are those individuals who took the survey. It's possible that this sample is representative of the whole industry, but it's equally possible that it isn't. So, think of this book as a guide; it points to trends and suggests themes for future research, but we can't generalise from its findings.

Nikandre Kopcke was born in Berlin and raised in New York City. She attended the University of Edinburgh and the London School of Economics, where she trained as a sociologist in gender and development. Since 2012 she has been CEO of Mazí Mas [mazimas.co.uk], a London-based social enterprise restaurant that provides employment and training to women from migrant and refugee communities.

Introduction

Stefanie Posavec, data designer

The open-ended responses were my favourite responses to explore, particularly the question about the survey respondents' favourite Pantone colours. I think we were unprepared for the amount of sarcastic, cheeky comments and criticism we would receive about this question, and couldn't help but laugh at ourselves and the answers, as even these wayward comments captured a particular 'spirit' of a graphic designer.

The main thing that I've learned from this survey is that while designers are an independent, opinionated [and, dare I say it, mouthy] bunch when it comes to how we feel about our practice and our chosen field, this strong will doesn't always translate into higher wages or shorter hours. I hope that we can use this confident voice to remind our clients and a wider public that the service we provide is valuable and essential.

Stefanie Posavec is a London-based, American-born designer / illustrator who works mainly in data-related design. Her client-commissioned work ranges from data visualisation and information design to commissioned data art. Often applying a handcrafted approach, her personal work focuses on the visual or physical representation of data derived from language, literature or scientific topics.

Introduction

How to use this book

Section title

Survey question pages relate to

Sample group, where appropriate

Symbol indicating where pages relate

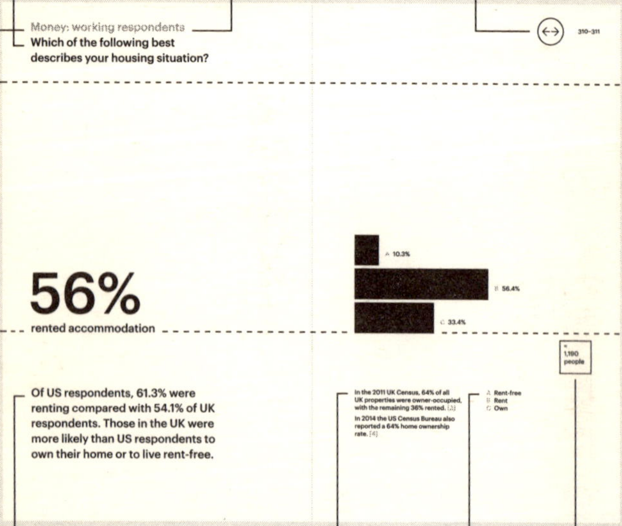

Commentary

Zone for main graphic, see examples on following pages

Comparator data providing useful benchmarks

Keys

Number of people / answers vary as not everyone answered every question

Notes

Percentages may not always total 100 due to rounding.

The same data is sometimes used in multiple places in order to examine it from a different perspective.

Examples

There are five main types of graphic used to represent the data in this book, as well as pages that show the results in words or percentages.

The following five examples use the same data from a fictitious sample group of 200 people. As you can see, the way this information is treated graphically has a bearing on how it is interpreted.

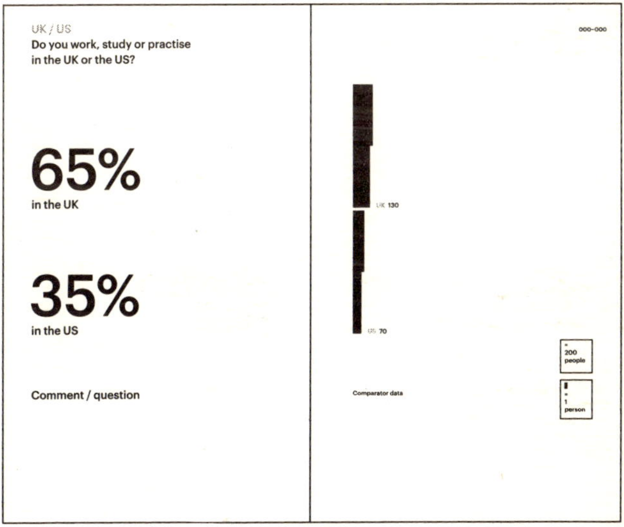

Example 1
Blocks of individuals

These chunky graphs help convey the people behind the data: they may look a bit like bar charts but they are actually made up of individual units representing each person in the data set.

These are only used when the data is being split into two, or in some cases four, major groups: anything more complex loses legibility in this form.

Examples

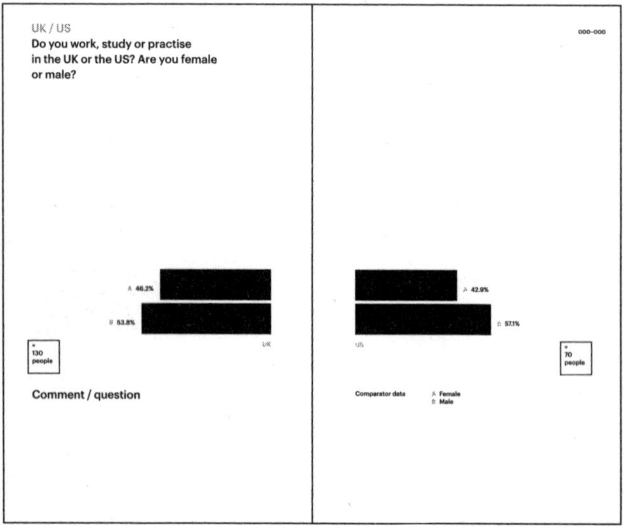

Example 2
Bar charts

Our most frequently used graphic is a bar chart. Here, 85mm width and 30pt height always represents 100%, with answers split across the page [along the y-axis, if you want to be technical].

The basic bar charts are sometimes divided by another data set; here, tints within each bar represent the further breakdown of the sample group.

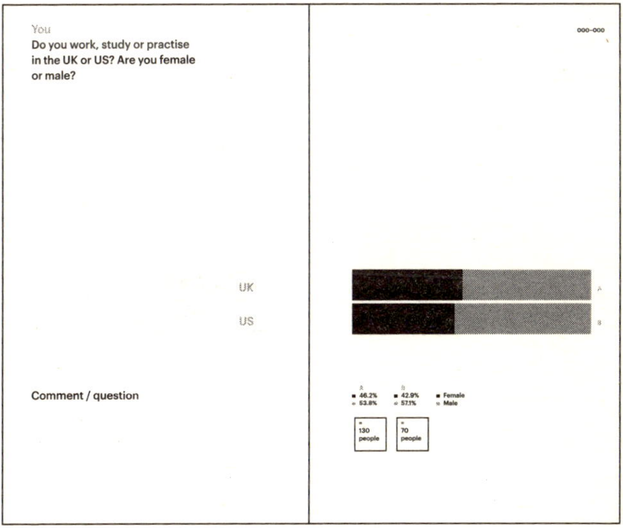

Example 3
Comparator bars

As with the bar charts, 85mm width and 30pt height always represents 100%. However, here the solid bars are divided by tints rather than split across the page, in order to compare different groups of respondents.

The bar labels on the left-hand page explain whose answers are captured in each bar.

Examples

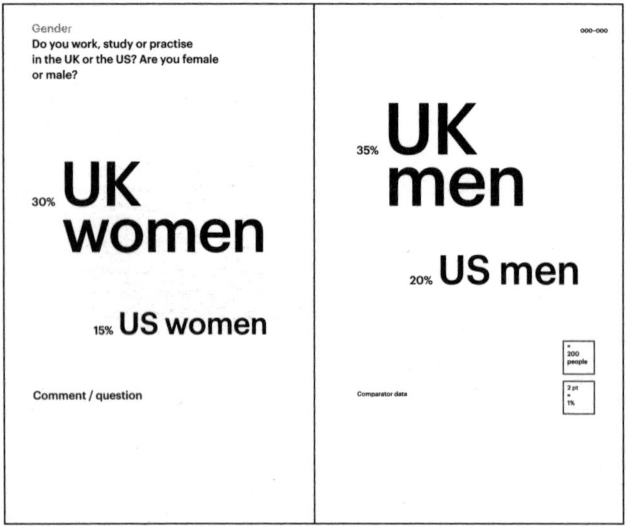

Example 4
Type size

Here, point size reflects the percentage of responses. These gesture at the size of response rather than being directly comparable – point size is not an accurate reflection of area, especially given different word lengths!

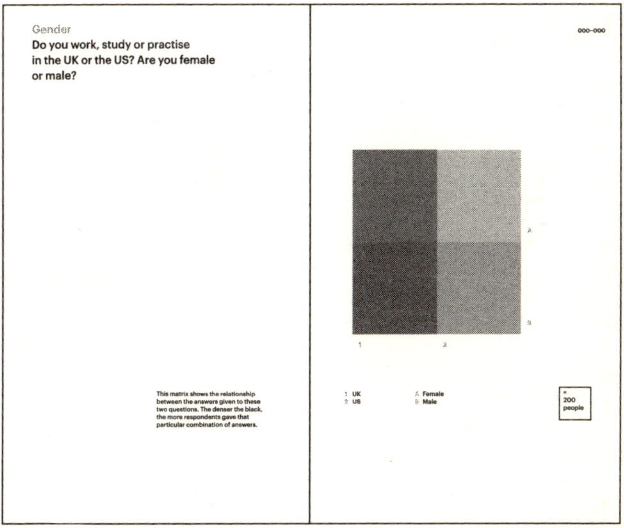

Example 5
Matrix

The matrices use tints of black to show percentages. They are used to show where certain combinations of responses were more common.

You

It would be easy to try and find the 'truth' about graphic designers in our data, but of course we don't know the full picture behind all the answers. For example, our sample group was substantially more UK-based than US-based, but there are not twice as many designers in Britain as in the States – rather, GraphicDesign& is based in the UK and our reach is likely bigger there. On the other hand, more men than women answered the survey, and it could be true that there are more men working in graphic design [in 2010 the Design Council estimated that 60% of UK designers were male]. [1]

What we can comment on with certainty is the make-up of the sample group who answered the survey, and as such who is captured in this book. The respondents were around two-thirds UK-based and one-third US-based [you can see some of the differences between those two populations on p056]. They were young [85% were under 40 years old], well-educated [88% had an undergraduate degree or higher], predominantly white [85%] and there were more male respondents than female.

Who answered the survey will affect how they answered, so this section sets out the basic demographics of everyone in the book. Of course, even this basic data is made up of individuals, each of whom Stefanie has elegantly captured on p034.

You

Who started the survey?

2,5

people

00

1pt
=
10
people

You

Who carried on with the survey?

1,9

people*

88

* 1,988 people filled in enough of the survey to be included in this book. If respondents answered whether they practised in the UK / US and stated their gender and / or their age, they were included.

1pt
=
10
people

You

Are you female or male? How old are you? What citizenship do you hold? What is the highest level of education you have successfully completed?

Sample group symbols

Stefanie Posavec, data designer

I wanted to create an information-rich family of symbols that would allow me to represent each individual survey respondent. These had to work in one colour and be visually distinct.

I hope the resulting patterned pages give a true sense of the number of people who took part and also show how diverse this group was. If you took the survey, try to find yourself – you were counted!

Sample group symbols

Gender

- ● Female
- ■ Male

Nationality

- ● ■ Citizen of country where survey was taken
- ○ □ Expatriate living in country where survey was taken
- ● ■ No nationality specified

Age

- ● ■ ≤20
- ● ■ 21–30
- ● ■ 31–40
- ● ■ 41–50
- ● ■ 51–60
- ● ■ 61+
- ▨ ▨ No age specified

Over the following pages, every person who told us where they practised and their gender is represented by a symbol comprised of a combination of the components shown here.

Level of education

- Secondary / high school or lower
- Further education / community college
- Undergraduate
- Postgraduate or higher
- No level of education specified

Example symbols

Female citizen
≤20
Education unknown

Male expatriate
≤20
Secondary / high school or lower

Female [nationality unknown]
21–30
Postgraduate or higher

Male expatriate
Age unknown
Postgraduate or higher

Female [nationality unknown]
Age unknown
No level of education specified

The age groups in this graphic are slightly different to those used across the rest of the book.

= 1,980 people

You

Sample group symbols: UK

Age ≤20

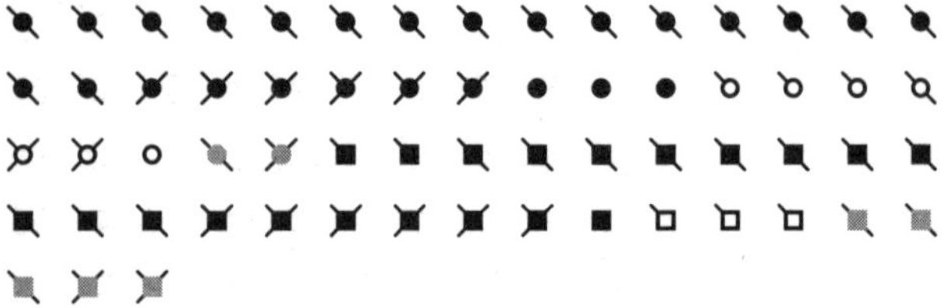

Age 21–30

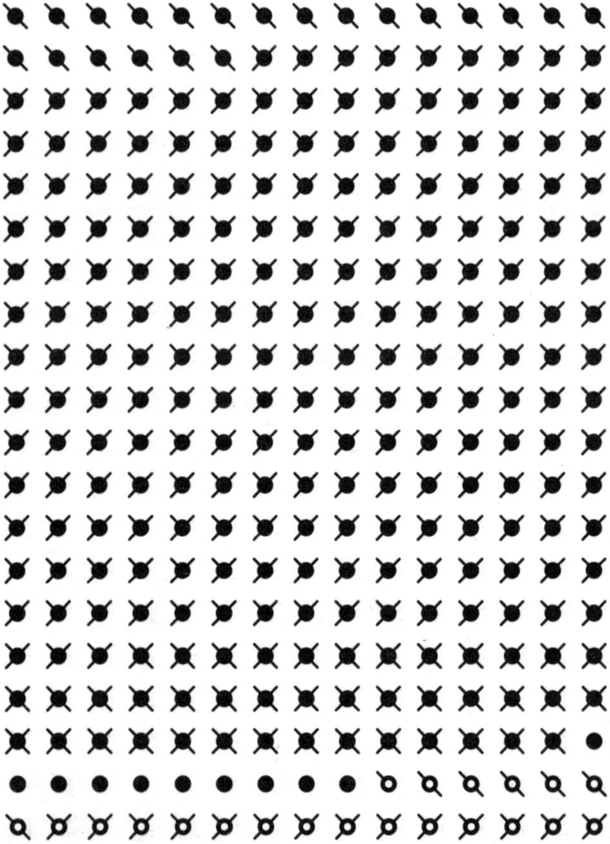

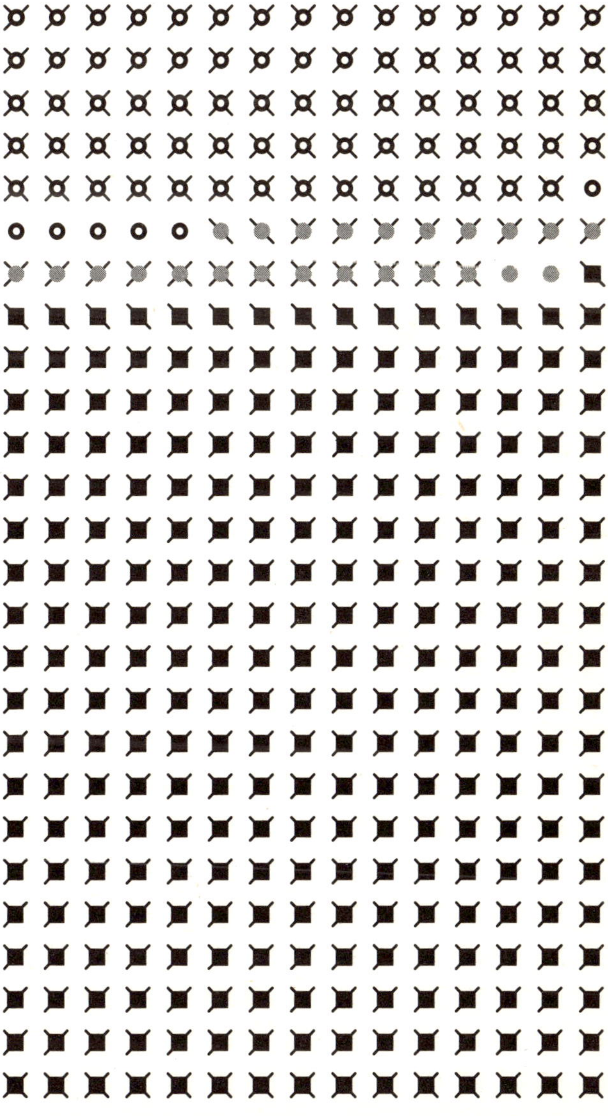

Sample group symbols: UK [continued]

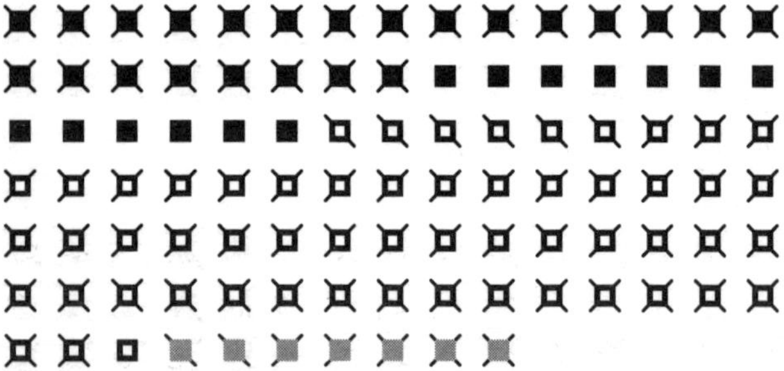

Age 31–40

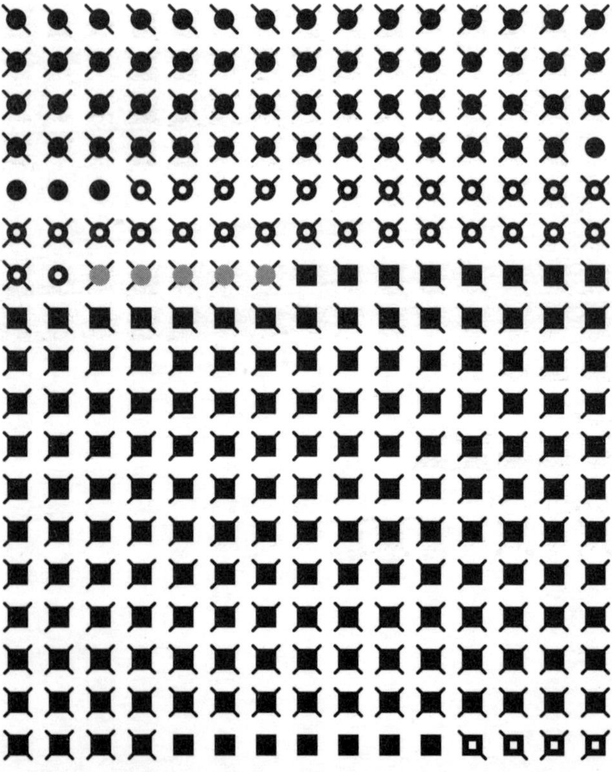

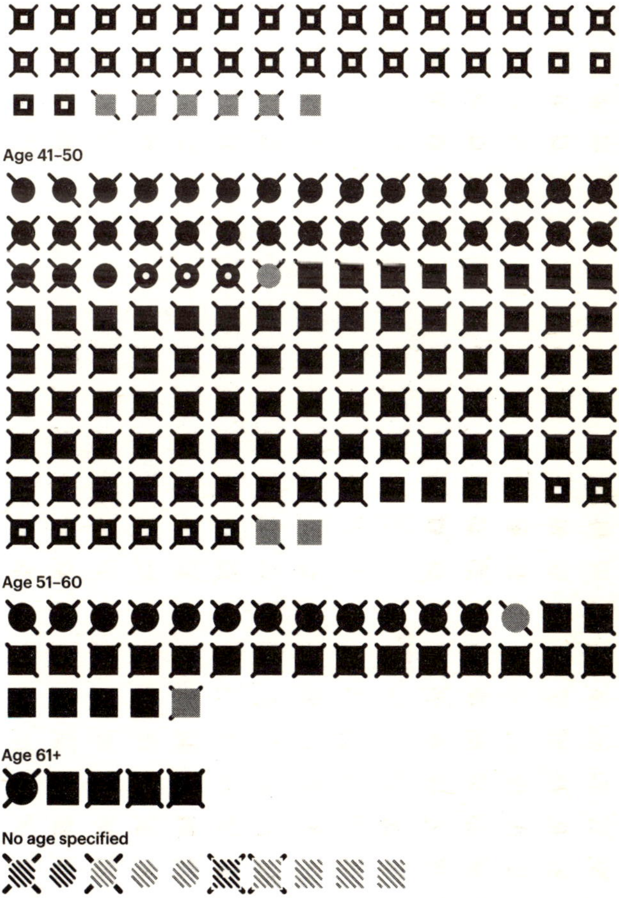
Age 41–50
Age 51–60
Age 61+
No age specified

You

Sample group symbols: US

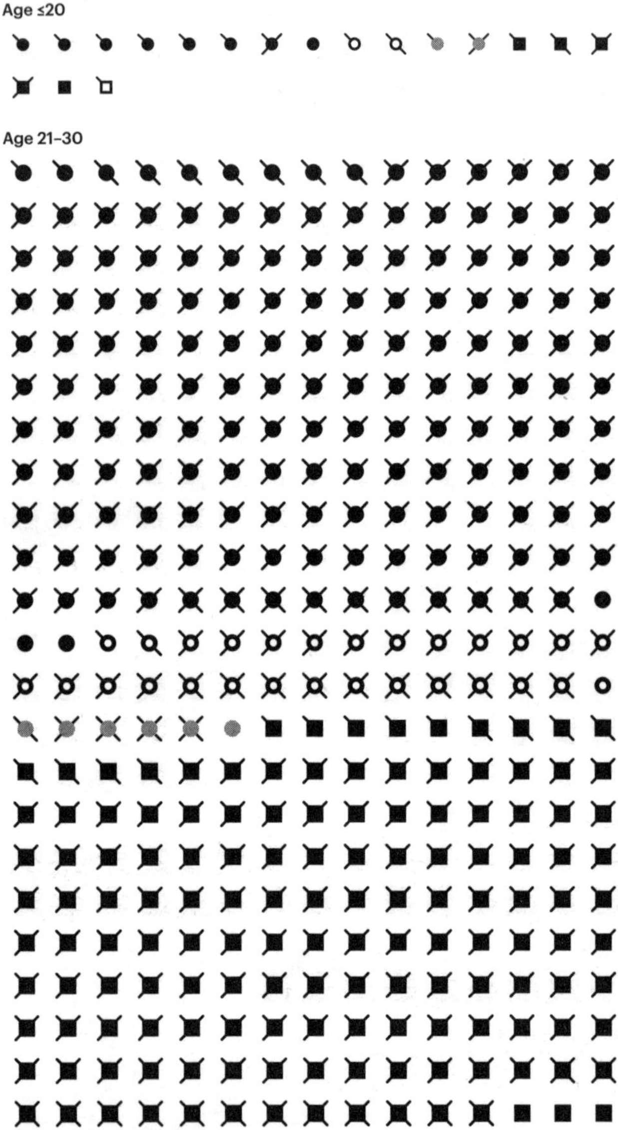

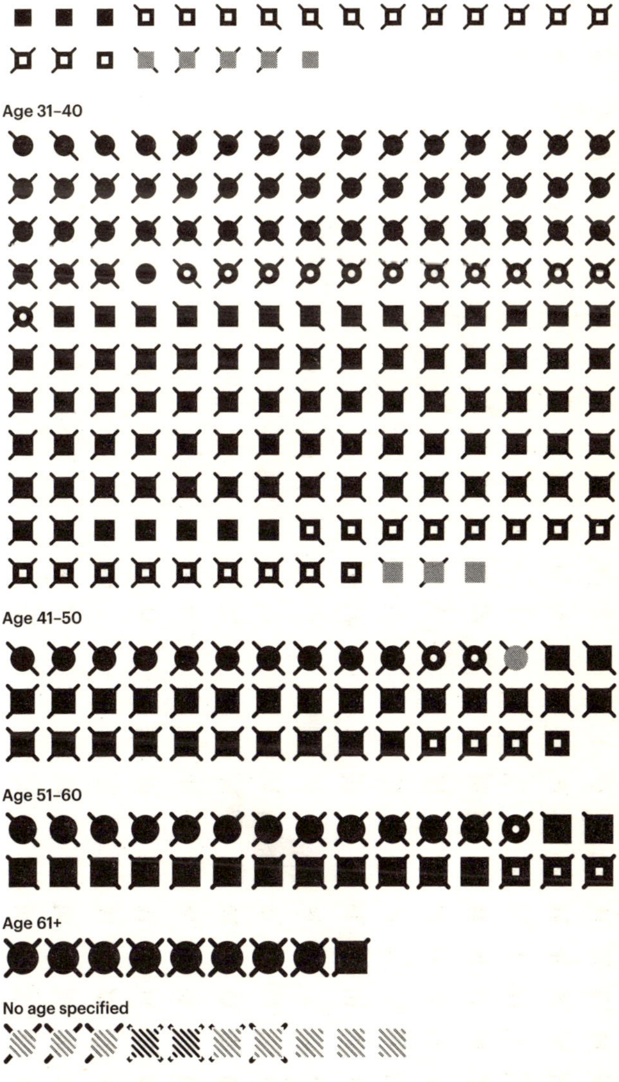
Age 31–40
Age 41–50
Age 51–60
Age 61+
No age specified

You

Do you work, study or practise in the UK or the US?

68%

in the UK

32%

in the US

Because more UK-based designers responded, where we show statistics about the whole sample group they will be more representative of the UK.

= 1,988 people

= 1 person

In 2014 there were approximately 64.6 million people living in the UK. [2] In 2015 there were approximately 322 million people living in the US. [3]

You

Are you female or male?

46%

female

54%

male

GD& wonders...

Do more men than women work in graphic design?

= 1,980 people

▮ = 1 person

In 2010 the Design Council estimated that 60% of all UK designers were male. The same report estimated that 84% of UK architects were male. [4]

You

How old are you?

60+	0.8%
50s	4.1%
40s	10%
30s	26.9%
20s	56.6%
<20	1.6%

Overall, our sample group was young: 85.1% of respondents were under 40.

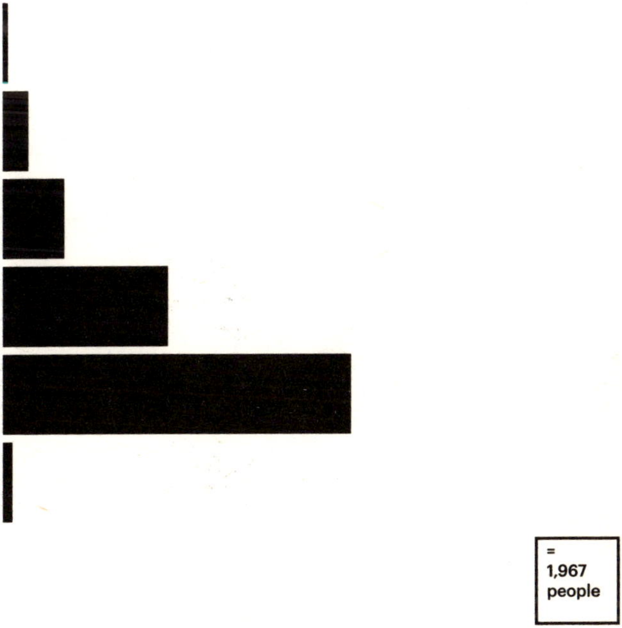

The modal [most common] age for respondents was 25. The average age was 30.

You

What is your ethnic group?

Asian	5.5%
Black	1.5%
Latino/a	2.7%
Mixed / multiple	3%
White	84.6%
Other	2.8%

This question has different standard answers in the UK and the US, see p064 for UK and p066 for US ethnic profiles.

You

What is the highest level of education you have successfully completed?

88%

undergraduate degree or higher

GD& wonders...

Do you need a degree to pursue a career in graphic design?

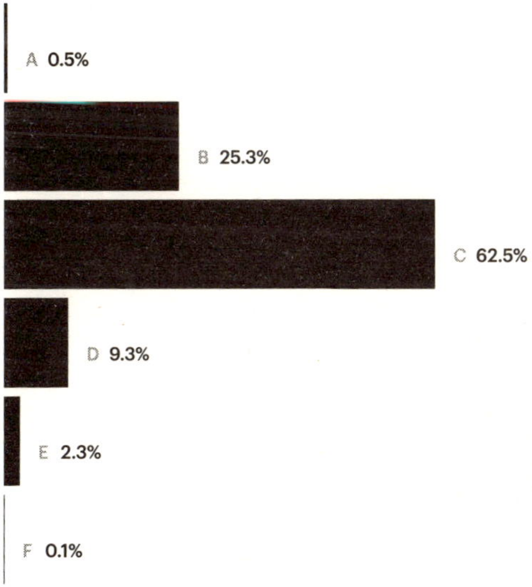

■ = 1,889 people

In 2012 the Office for National Statistics reported that 27.2% of UK citizens [aged 16–74] held an undergraduate degree or higher. [5]

In 2014 the US Census Bureau reported that 29.3% of US citizens [aged 18+] held an undergraduate degree or higher. [6]

- A Doctorate
- B Postgraduate qualification or degree
- C Undergraduate degree
- D Further education / community college
- E Secondary / high school
- F Primary / middle school

You

Which of the following best describes your current occupation?

Paid a salary / wage	54.7%
Doing freelance work	15.4%
Partner in / running own business	12.4%
Student or intern	11.4%
Educator / academic	4%
Managing a business	1.1%
Not in work	1.1%

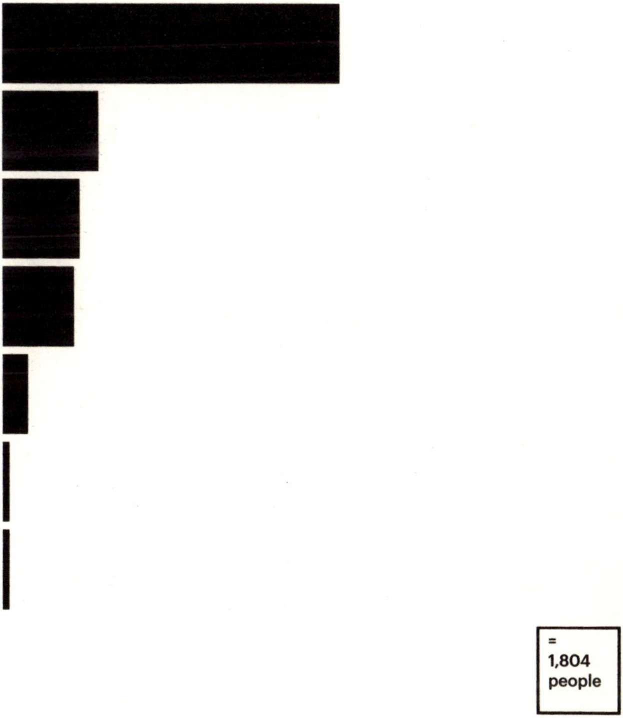

At this point in the survey respondents were split according to their answer and asked different questions relevant to their occupation.

UK / US

Nikandre Kopcke

The UK and the US are very different places to live, work, and raise families. The US has less social provisioning and fewer work-related benefits and protections than the UK; healthcare is still largely privatised and there is no statutory requirement for paid sick leave, annual leave, or maternity leave.

In practice this means that Americans are used to forking out for basic services that Britons take for granted. Americans also tend to work longer hours to pay for these benefits. A 2014 Gallup poll put the average full-time work week in the US at 47 hours, [1] nearly 30% higher than the current UK average of 37 hours. [2] Full-time private sector employees in the US average just 10 days of paid leave per year [3] compared to the 28 legally guaranteed to full-time employees in the UK.

No surprise, then, that our US respondents reported working more hours on average than our UK respondents. What we found interesting was that national differences in work habits seemed to translate to a difference in attitudes toward work-life balance. While both UK- and US-based designers reported working more hours than they were paid to, the Americans were on the whole less bothered about this than the Brits, possibly because there is a greater cultural expectation of long work hours in the US.

The results suggest that on the whole, designers in the UK felt less satisfied with their work life than designers in the US. Financial security was more of an issue for UK-based designers, especially the lowest-earning ones, and overall career satisfaction was lower [though women in both groups were more satisfied than men]. Whether this is evidence of a more challenging work environment in the UK, or simply a matter of reality falling short of UK designers' higher expectations, is a question for future research.

UK / US

Do you work, study or practise in the UK or the US?

US 631

= 1,960 people

▮ = 1 person

Respondents were included in this section if they answered whether they practised in the UK / US and stated both their gender and their age.

This means that the sample group here is slightly smaller than that shown on p045.

UK / US

Are you female or male?

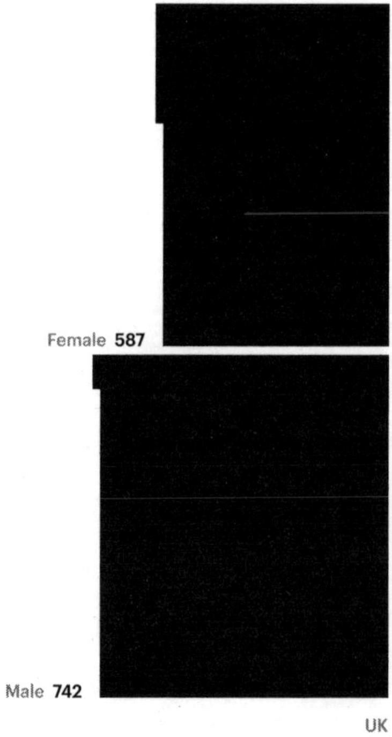

There was a more equal gender distribution among US respondents [48.8% female, 51.2% male] than among UK respondents [44.2% female, 55.8% male].

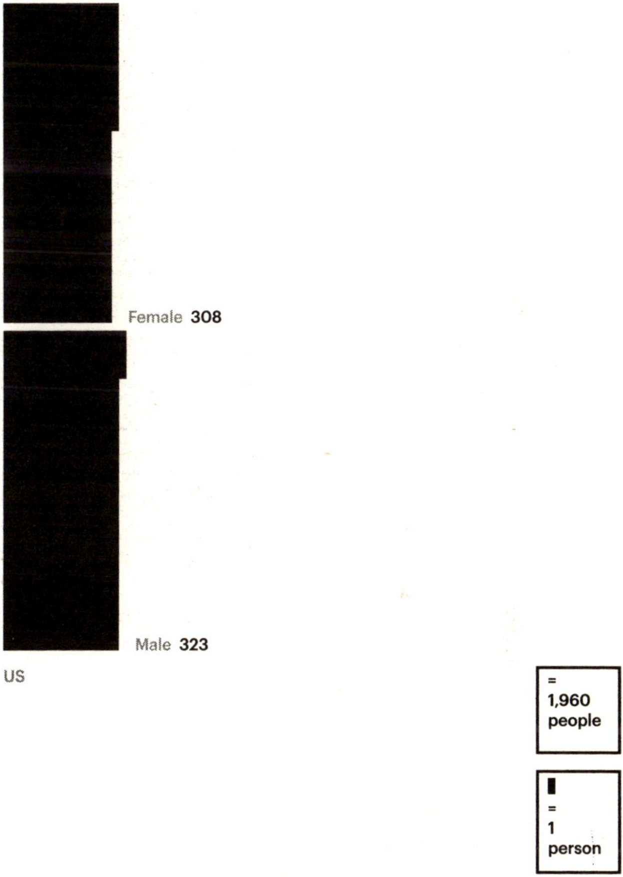
Female 308
Male 323
US
= 1,960 people
= 1 person

UK / US

How old are you?

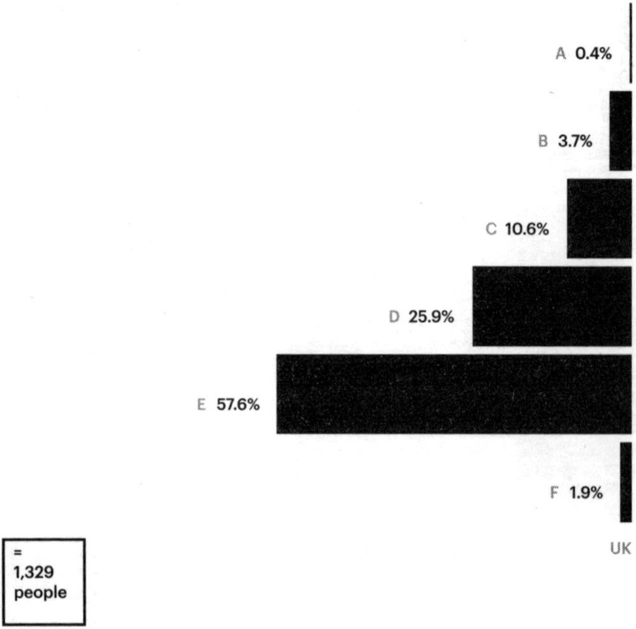

The sample group based in the US was slightly older.

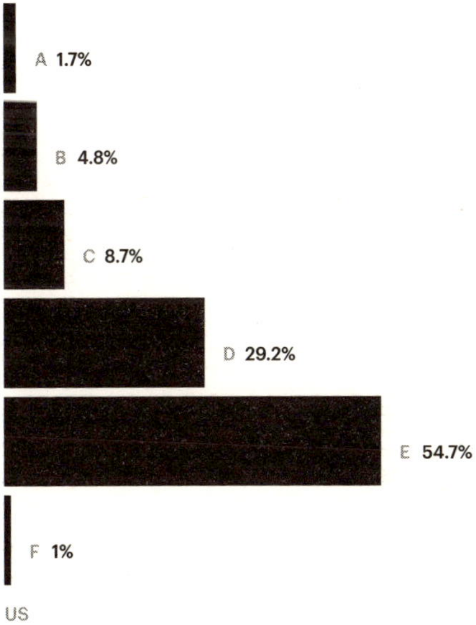

= 631 people

In 2014 the UK Office for National Statistics estimated the median age in the UK to be 40 years old. [4]

In 2010 the US Census found the median age in the US to be 37.2 years old. [5]

A 60+
B 50s
C 40s
D 30s
E 20s
F <20

UK / US: UK

What is your ethnic group?

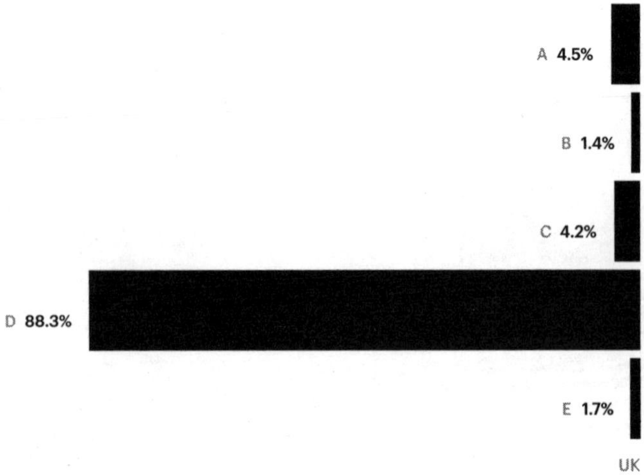

1.4% of UK respondents were Black / African / Caribbean, compared with 3.3% of the general UK population.

(+→) 064–065

UK

88%

white

= 1,321 people

	General UK population [6]
7.5%	Asian / Asian British
3.3%	Black / African / Caribbean
2.2%	Mixed / multiple
86%	White
1%	Other

A Asian
B Black / African / Caribbean
C Mixed / multiple
D White
E Other

UK / US: US

What is your ethnic group?

US

79%

white

1.8% of US respondents were Black / African American, compared with 13.2% of the general US population.

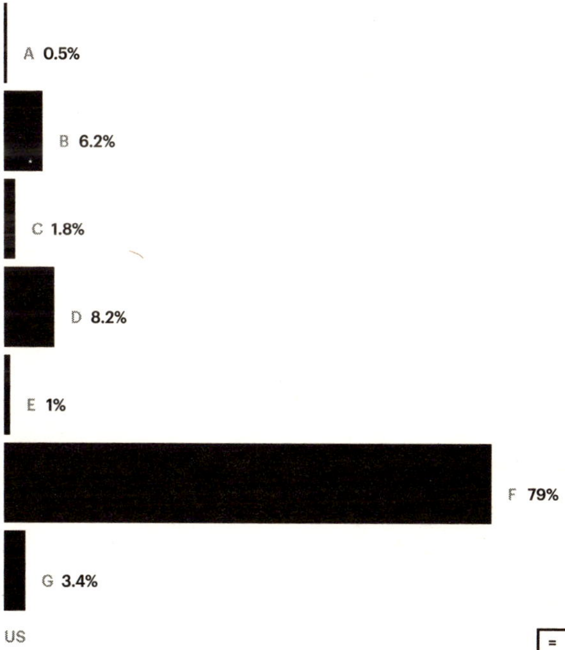

= 625 people

General US population [7]

1.2%	American Indian / Eskimo
5.3%	Asian
13.2%	Black / African American
0.2%	Pacific Islander
77.7%	White
2.4%	Two or more races

A **American Indian / Eskimo**
B **Asian**
C **Black**
D **Latino/a**
E **Pacific Islander**
F **White**
G **Other**

UK / US

What citizenship do you hold?

UK

American, Australian, Austrian, Bangladeshi, Belgian, British, Bruneian, Bulgarian, Canadian, Croatian, Cypriot, Danish, Dutch, European*, Finnish, French, German, Greek, Hong Kong [Chinese], Hungarian, Indian, Indonesian, Iranian, Irish, Israeli, Italian, Korean, Latvian, Lebanese, Lithuanian, Malaysian, Maltese, Mexican, New Zealand, Norwegian, Pakistani, Peruvian, Polish, Portuguese, Romanian, Russian, Singaporean, Slovenian, South African, Spanish, Swedish, Swiss, Thai, Turkish, Venezuelan, Vietnamese

□ = 1,280 people

Some respondents held double or even triple citizenship.

US

American, Argentinian, Australian, Brazilian, British, Canadian, Chinese, Colombian, Dominican, Dutch, Egyptian, Finnish, French, Hong Kong [Chinese], Hungarian, Irish, Israeli, Italian, Lebanese, Macau [Chinese], Mexican, Russian, Singaporean, South Korean, Spanish, Swedish, Swiss, Costa Rican, Trinidadian, Portuguese, Turkish, Venezuelan

= 615 people

* We know this isn't an official citizenship, but enough people stated it to warrant inclusion!

UK / US

What is the highest level of education you have successfully completed?

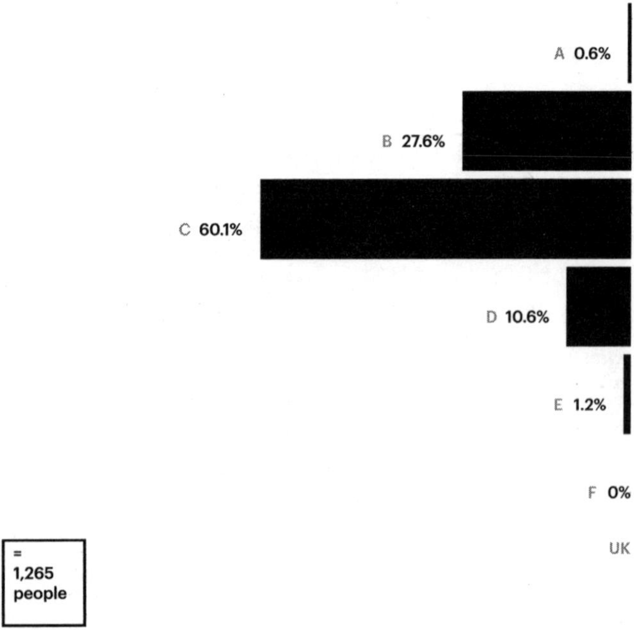

UK respondents reported a higher level of academic achievement than those in the US.

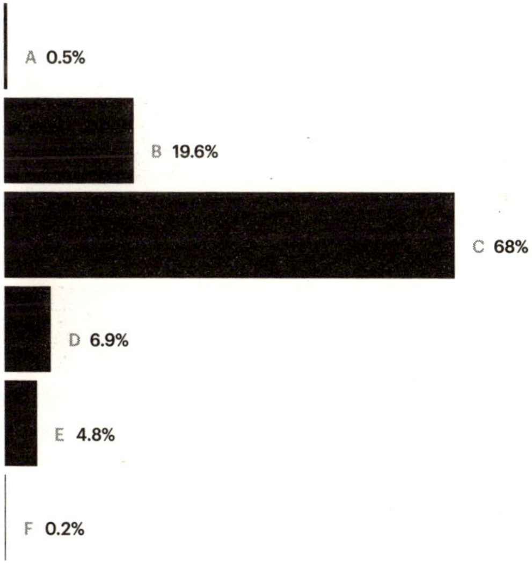

US

= 606 people

A Doctorate

B Postgraduate qualification or degree

C Undergraduate degree

D Further education / community college

E Secondary / high school

F Primary / middle school

UK / US

What is your annual income before tax?

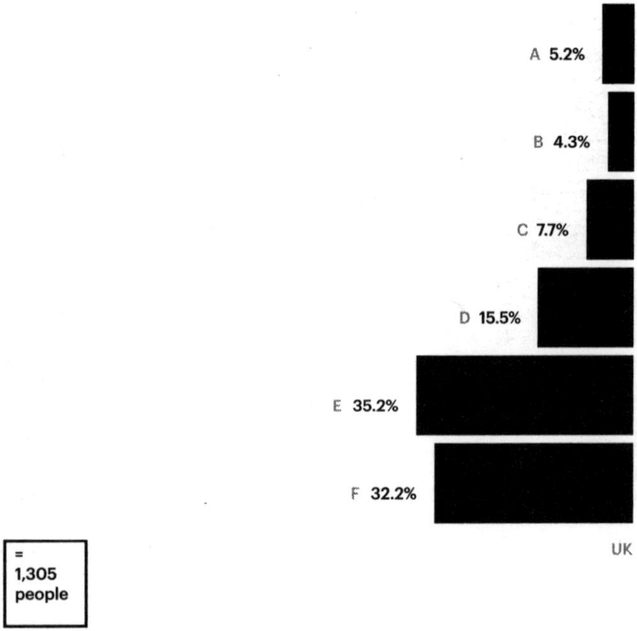

US incomes were more evenly distributed; the UK had a higher proportion of respondents earning in the lowest two income brackets.

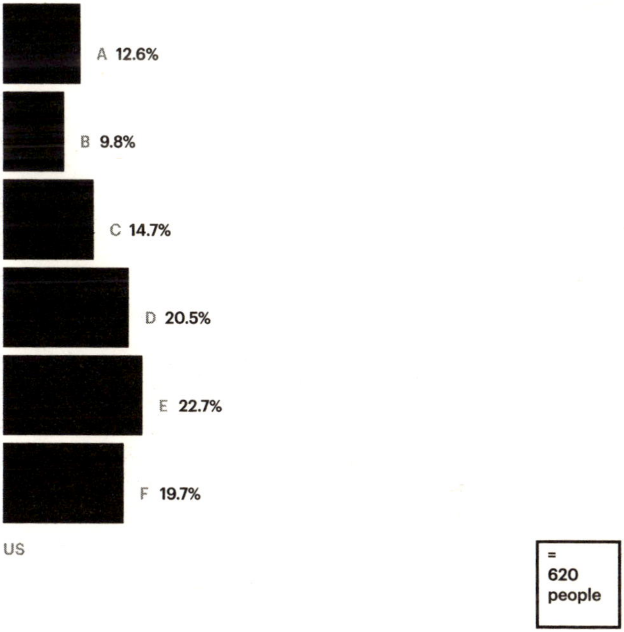

In 2012, the mean annual income in the UK was £28,800. [8]

In 2014, the mean annual income in the US was $47,230. [9]

Please note that UK / US income brackets, although roughly comparable, are not exactly equivalent.

A £60k+ / $90k+
B £50–60k / $75–90k
C £40–50k / $60–75k
D £30–40k / $45–60k
E £20–30k / $30–45k
F <£20k / <$30k

UK / US

What is your annual income before tax?

UK

67%

£30k or less per year

10%

more than £50k per year

= 1,305 people

US

42%

$45k or less per year

22%

more than $75k per year

■ =
620
people

UK / US

Which of the following best describes how you feel about your / your family's present income? What is your annual income before tax?

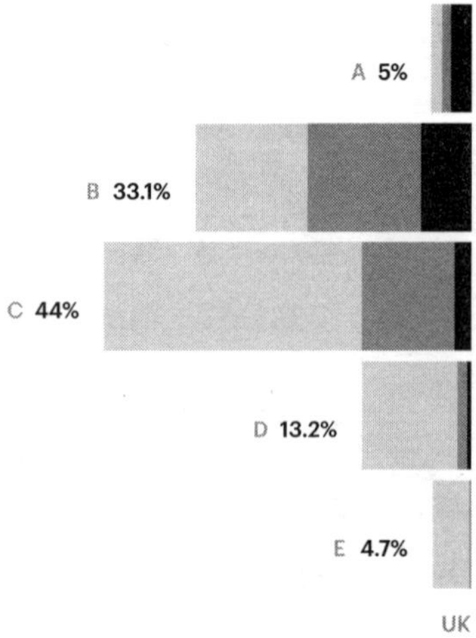

=
795
people

Proportionately more respondents on lower incomes were finding it hard in the UK, but proportionately more respondents on higher incomes were finding it hard in the US.

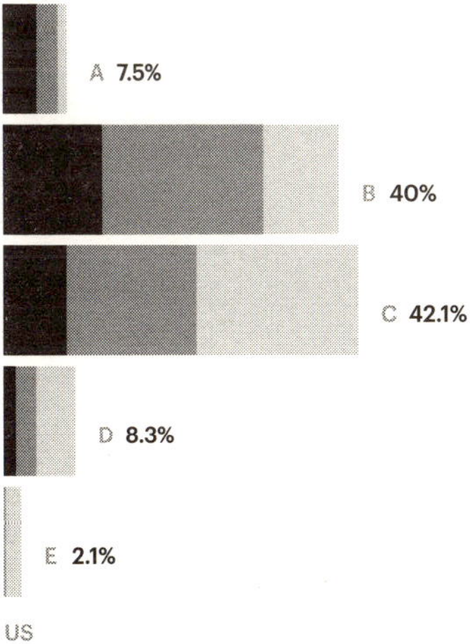

= 375 people

A Living very comfortably on present income
B Living comfortably on present income
C Getting by on present income
D Finding it difficult on present income
E Finding it very difficult on present income

UK	US
■ £50k+	■ $75k+
▒ £30–50k	▒ $45–75k
░ <£30k	░ <$45k

UK / US

Which of the following best describes how you feel about your / your family's present income?

UK

18%

found it difficult to manage on present income

38%

were comfortable

= 795 people

US

10%

found it difficult to manage on present income

48%

were comfortable

=
375
people

UK / US: under 40

What is your annual income before tax?

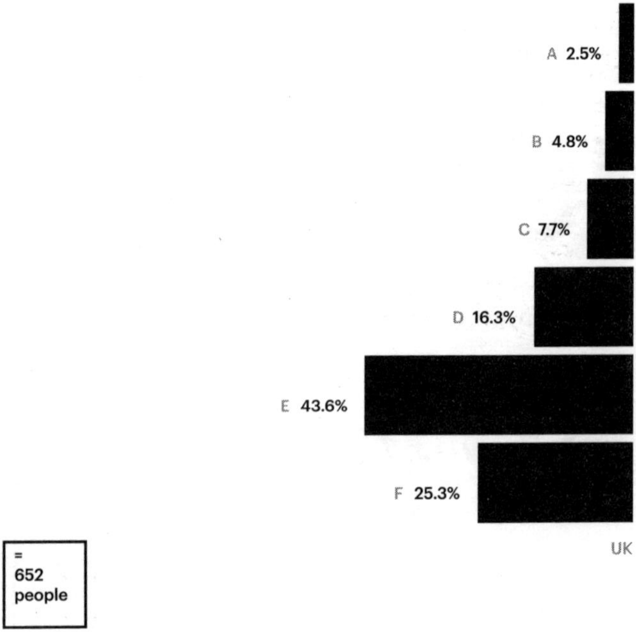

85.1% of respondents were under 40. In this group, the UK respondents tended to earn less than their US counterparts.

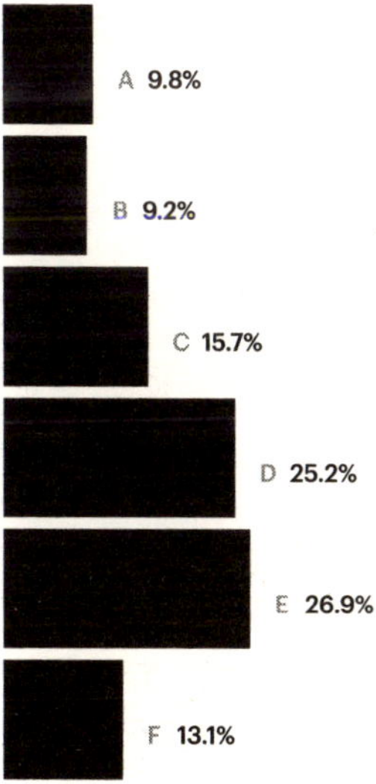

US

= 305 people

Please note that UK / US income brackets, although roughly comparable, are not exactly equivalent.

A £60k+ / $90k+
B £50–60k / $75–90k
C £40–50k / $60–75k
D £30–40k / $45–60k
E £20–30k / $30–45k
F <£20k / <$30k

UK / US

Generally, how many hours do you work in a week?

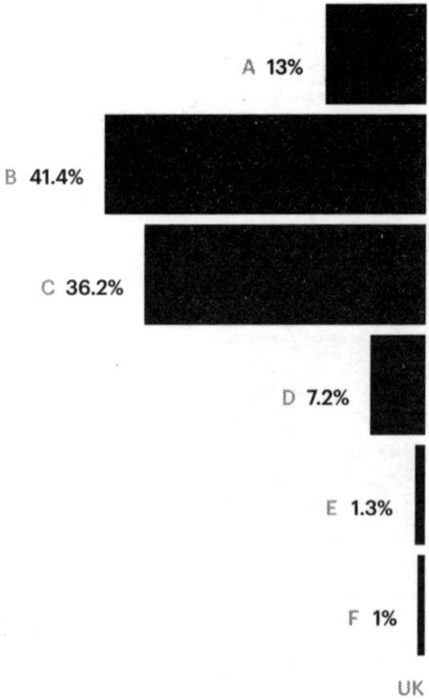

= 839 people

US respondents reported working longer hours than their UK counterparts.

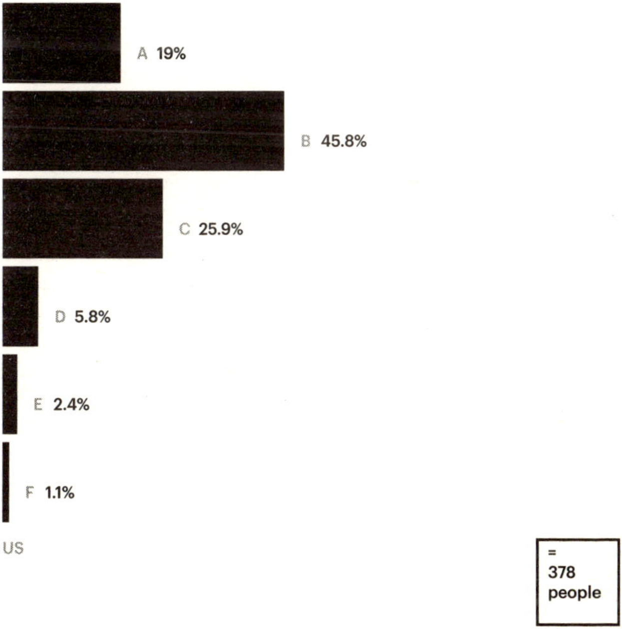

In 2015 the Office for National Statistics reported that the average working week of all UK workers was 32 hours. [10]

In 2015 the Bureau of Labor Statistics reported that the average working week of all US employees was 35 hours. [11]

See p056 for full-time working week statistics.

A 50+ hours
B 41–50 hours
C 36–40 hours
D 22–35 hours
E 16–21 hours
F <16 hours

UK / US

Would you prefer to work more or fewer hours than you presently work?

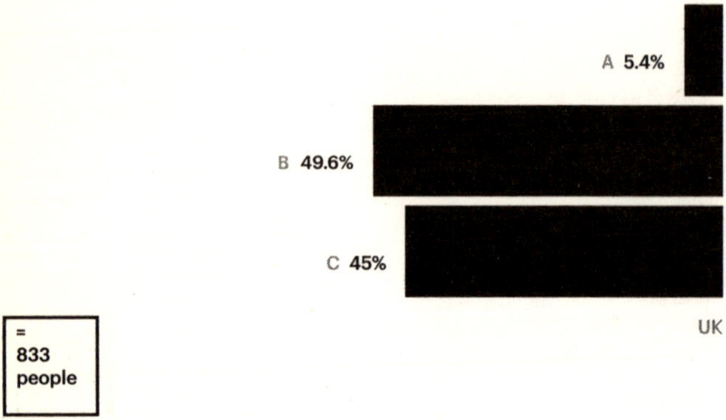

Perhaps unsurprisingly, not many respondents wanted to work more hours, but a substantial number would choose to work fewer hours.

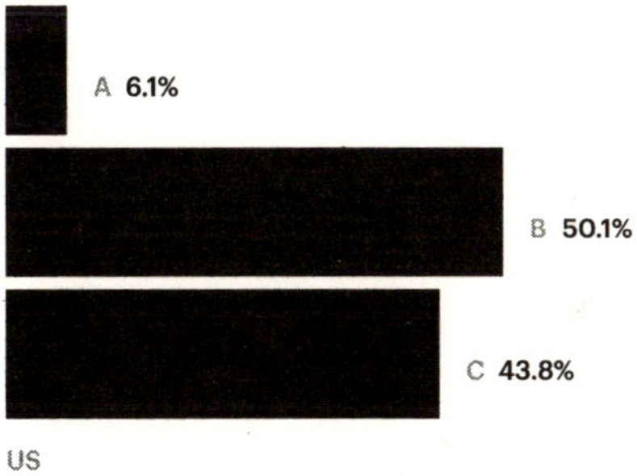

= 379 people

A I would prefer to work more hours

B I'm happy with the hours I work

C I would prefer to work fewer hours

UK / US

Generally, how many hours do you work in a week? Would you prefer to work more or fewer hours than you presently work?

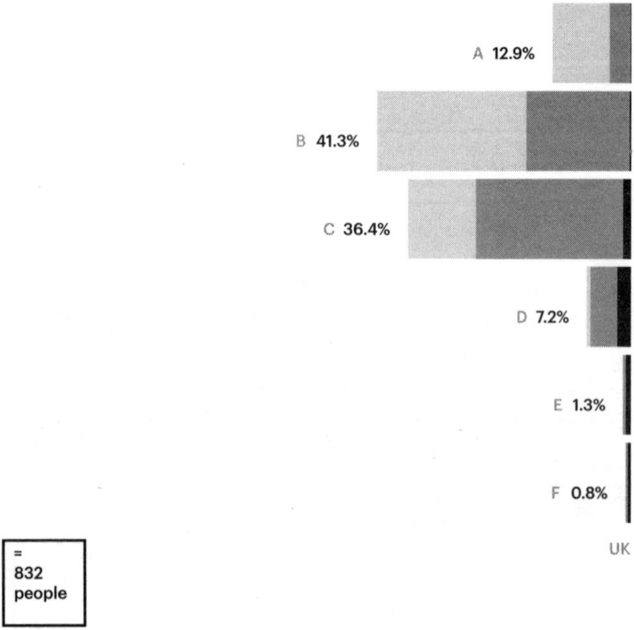

Even among those working more than 50 hours in a week, a few respondents would have liked more time at work!

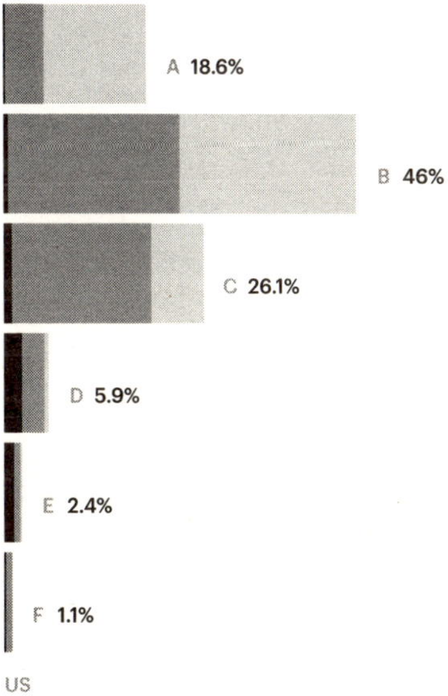

= 376 people

A 50+ hours
B 41–50 hours
C 36–40 hours
D 22–35 hours
E 16–21 hours
F <16 hours

■ I would prefer to work more hours

■ I'm happy with the hours I work

■ I would prefer to work fewer hours

UK / US

Do you work more hours than you are paid to work?

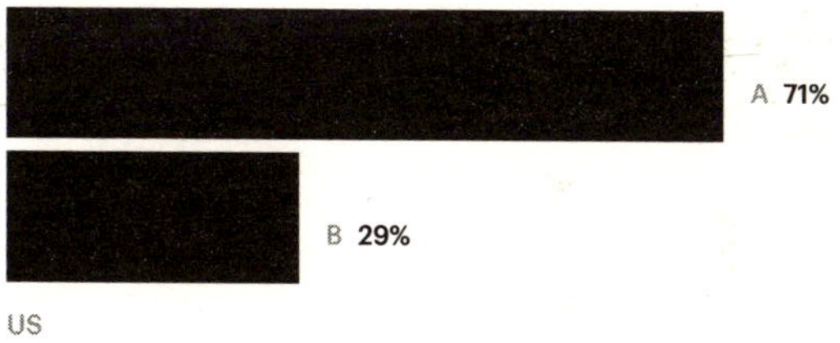

= 451 people

A Yes
B No

UK / US: work 50+ hours per week

Which of the following best describes your current occupation?

	UK
Doing freelance work	18.5%
Educator / academic	10.2%
Managing a business	2.8%
Paid a wage / salary	42.6%
Partner in a business	5.6%
Running own business	20.4%

= 108 people

In the UK, a larger proportion of respondents working more than 50 hours were freelancers.

US

6.9%	Doing freelance work
6.9%	Educator / academic
1.4%	Managing a business
63.9%	Paid a wage / salary
8.3%	Partner in a business
12.5%	Running own business

□ = 72 people

UK / US: work 40+ hours per week

What is your annual income before tax?

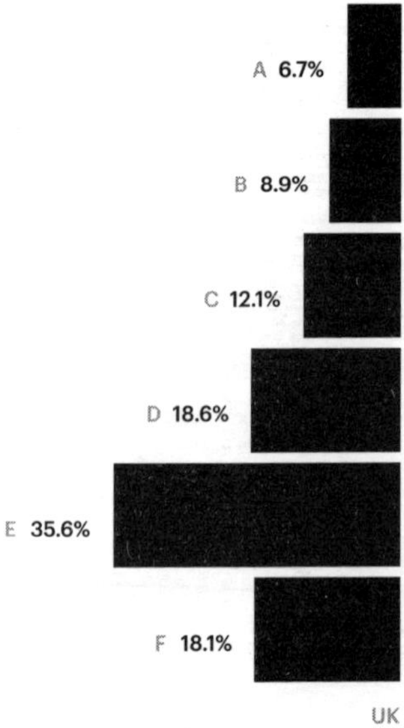

= 447 people

GD& wonders...
Are longer hours financially rewarding because those that can, take on more projects? Or because more hours are expected at a higher level?

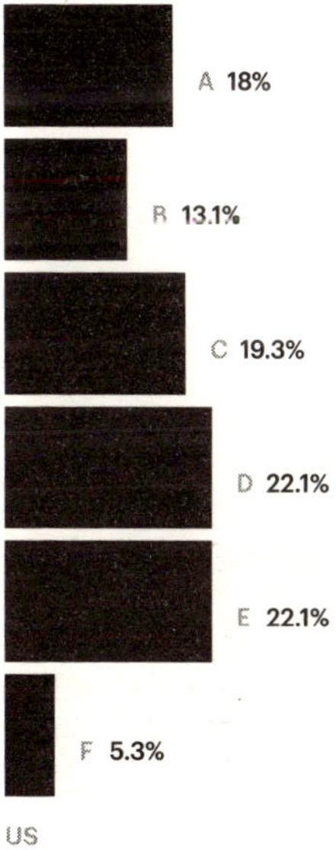

= 244 people

Respondents working more than 40 hours in a week were earning more than the general sample group – see p072 for comparison.

Please note that UK / US income brackets, although roughly comparable, are not exactly equivalent.

A £60k+ / $90k+
B £50–60k / $75–90k
C £40–50k / $60–75k
D £30–40k / $45–60k
E £20–30k / $30–45k
F <£20k / <$30k

UK / US

Do you do free pitching / speculative work?

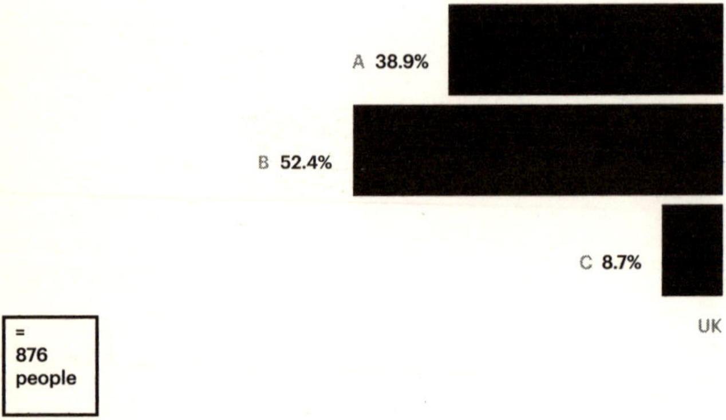

GD& wonders...

Are US respondents less likely to do free pitching because they are under less pressure to do so?

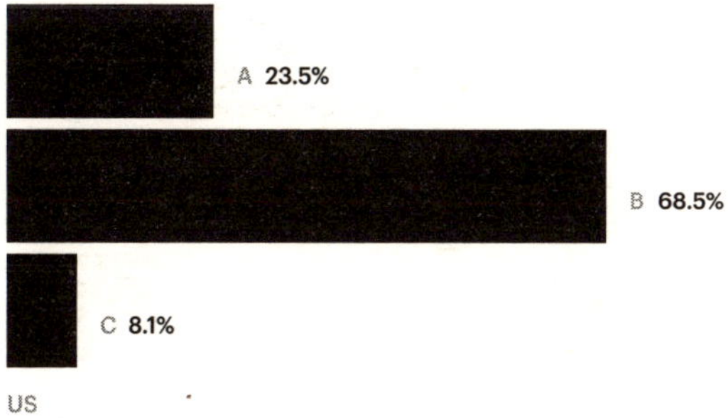

= 447 people

A Yes
B No
C Don't know

UK / US

Do you agree with free pitching / speculative work?

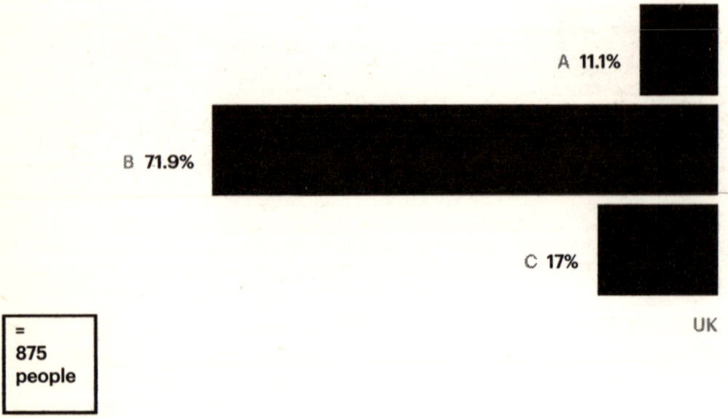

Both UK and US respondents largely disagreed with free pitching.

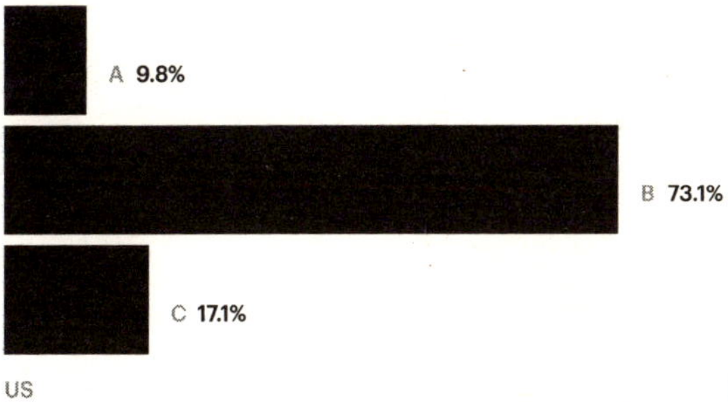

= 449 people

A Yes
B No
C Don't know

UK / US

Do you do free pitching? Do you agree with free pitching?

UK

52%

didn't do free pitching but

72%

disagreed with it

= 876 people

= 875 people

In general, US and UK respondents were united in their opposition to free pitching, but US respondents had more consistency between practice and principle.

US

69%

didn't do free pitching but

73%

disagreed with it

= 447 people

= 449 people

UK / US

Please list any professional organisations you are a member of.

15.7% D&AD

8.2% ISTD

7.5% AGI

6% AOI

5.2% DBA

4.5% The Typographic Circle

3.7% RSA

= 134 answers

UK

GD& wonders...
Does the UK need an organisation like AIGA?

57.3% AIGA

6.3% ADC

4.2% TDC

US

=
192
answers

2pt
=
1%

Graphic shows all organisations listed by five or more respondents. There were many other organisations mentioned, including: AAF, Chartered Society of Designers, Society of Publication Designers, YCN, Society of Typographic Afficionados and Crack Team of International Space Commandos.

Gender

Nikandre Kopcke

I came to this project with an interest in exploring the gender dynamics of the graphic design industry. By that point I'd worked on two earlier projects with Lucienne and Rebecca and had spent a fair bit of time with women graphic designers. I was curious about something I'd heard repeated often: women outnumber men among graphic design graduates, and yet there are very few women at the top of the industry. Why?

This question interests me in every industry [unfortunately it tends to still be relevant in every industry], but I find it especially interesting in professions that rely on skills that have historically been considered feminine. Art and design, like cooking, are activities that at the amateur and lower professional levels are associated with women, but at the highest levels are overwhelmingly dominated by men.

What we found when we compared women's and men's responses to our survey surprised even me. Income inequality was stark across the board, with women designers in the US one and a half times more likely than men to be making less than $30k a year, and nearly twice *less* likely to be making more than $90k. The UK results were even more definitive: women were one and a half times more likely to be earning less than £20k, but *six* times less likely to be earning over £60k.

Measures of confidence cleaved along gender lines too. Men were more likely to think their work was better than that of others, to feel comfortable promoting it, and to volunteer to speak about it publicly. Women were more likely to sense inequality at work in the industry; they were much more likely than men to think graphic design had a masculine culture, and among UK-based designers women were much more likely to think that who you know most advantages people in the industry, whereas men thought success was down to hard work.

Gender

Are you female or male?

Female **895**

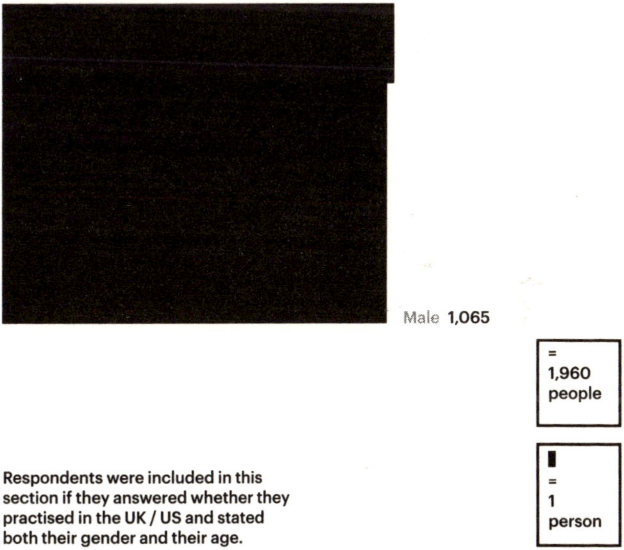

Respondents were included in this section if they answered whether they practised in the UK / US and stated both their gender and their age.

Gender

Do you work, study or practise in the UK or the US?

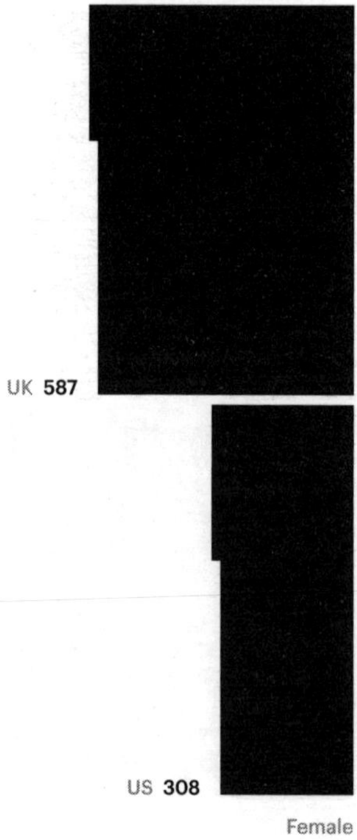

Male

= 1,960 people

= 1 person

Gender

How old are you?

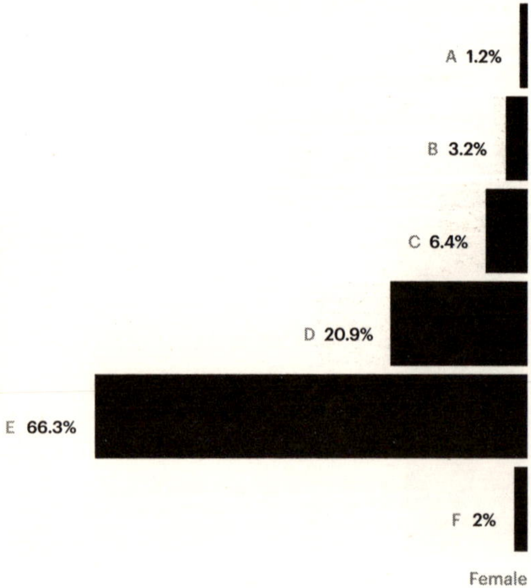

= 895 people

GD& wonders...
Why the women who responded to the survey were younger than the men.

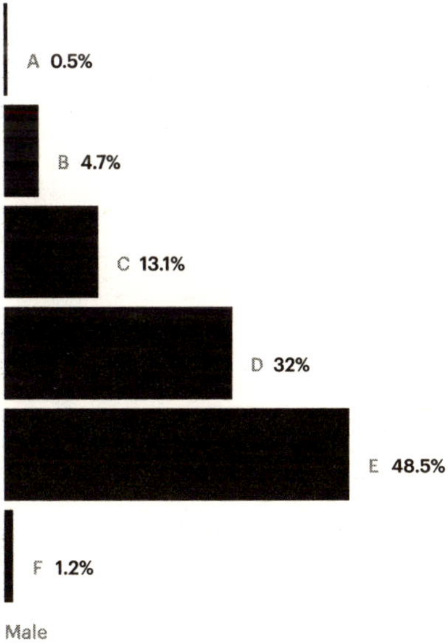

= 1,065 people

A 60+
B 50s
C 40s
D 30s
E 20s
F <20

Gender

What is the highest level of education you have successfully completed?

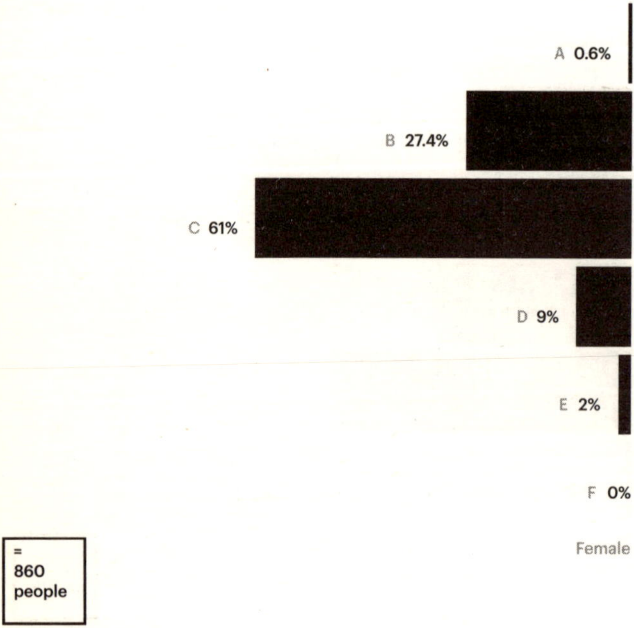

89% of women had an undergraduate degree or higher, compared with 87.4% of men.

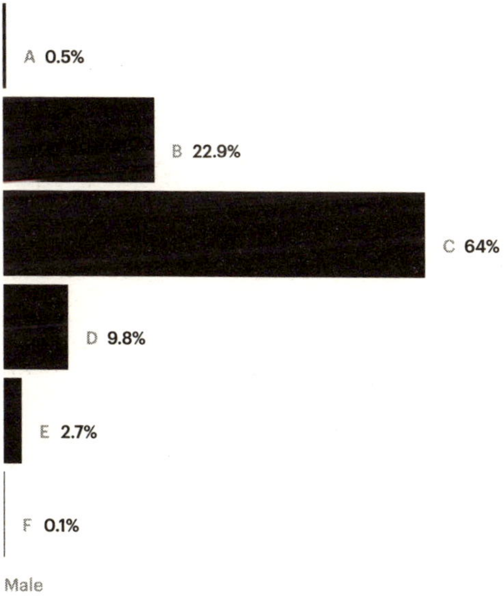

= 1,011 people

- A Doctorate
- B Postgraduate qualification or degree
- C Undergraduate degree
- D Further education / community college
- E Secondary / high school
- F Primary / middle school

Gender

What is your annual income before tax?

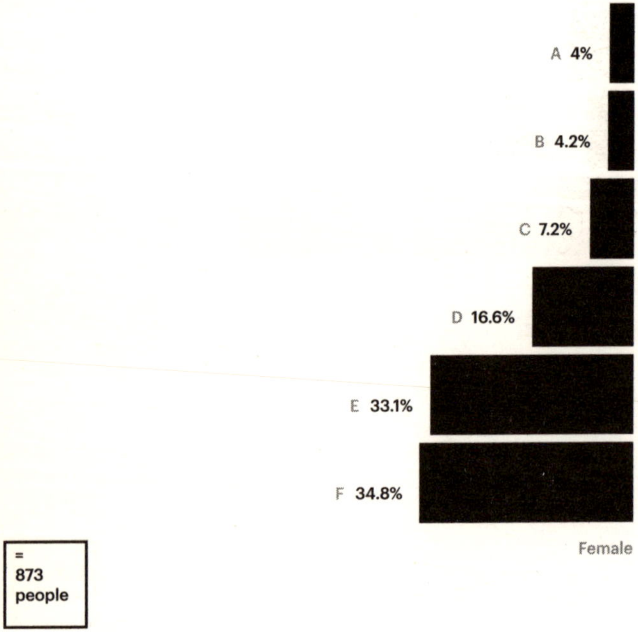

8.2% of women had an annual income of more than £50k / $75k, compared with 18.2% of men.

67.9% of women had an income of less than £30k / $45k, compared to 52.4% of men.

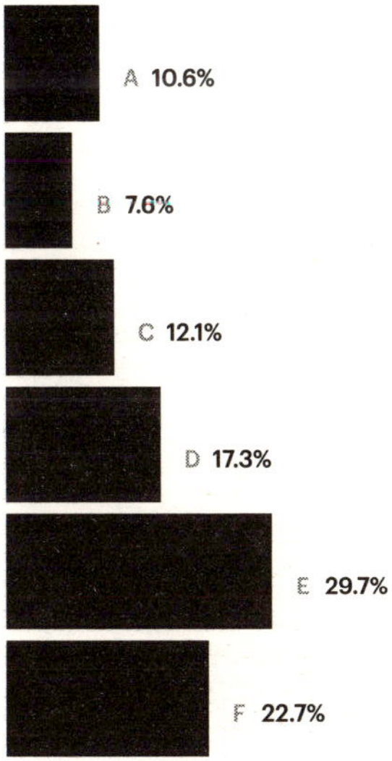

Male

= 1,046 people

Please note that UK / US income brackets, although roughly comparable, are not exactly equivalent.

A £60k+ / $90k+
B £50–60k / $75–90k
C £40–50k / $60–75k
D £30–40k / $45–60k
E £20–30k / $30–45k
F <£20k / <$30k

Gender: women

What is your annual income before tax?

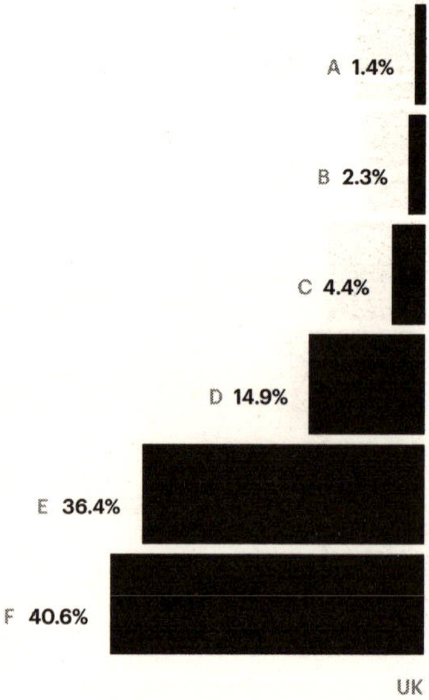

= 571 people

GD& wonders...
Is it better to be a female graphic designer in the US?

↔ 114–115

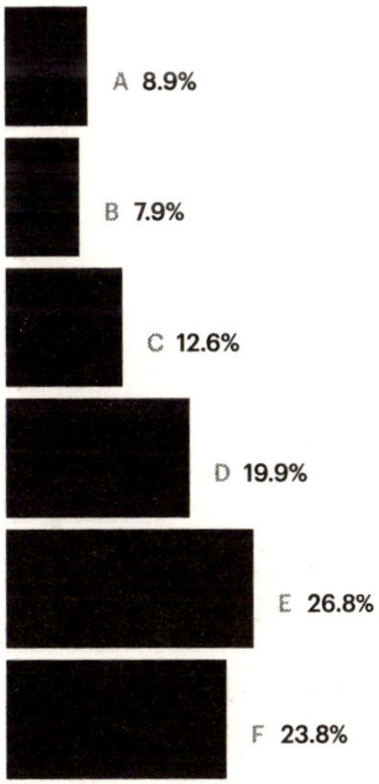

US

■ = 302 people

Please note that UK / US income brackets, although roughly comparable, are not exactly equivalent.

A £60k+ / $90k+
B £50–60k / $75–90k
C £40–50k / $60–75k
D £30–40k / $45–60k
E £20–30k / $30–45k
F <£20k / <$30k

Gender: men

What is your annual income before tax?

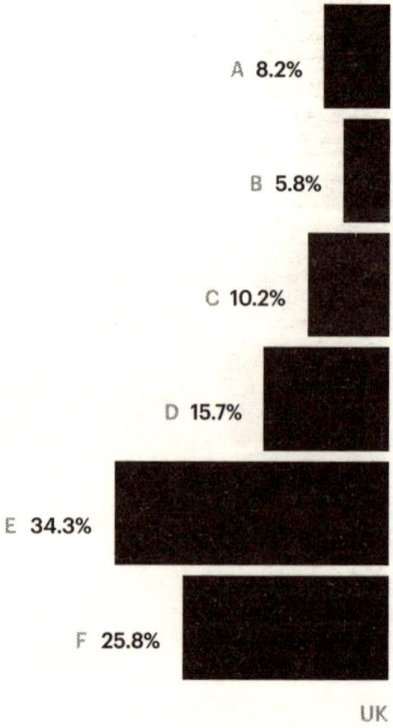

= 728 people

GD& wonders...
Is it better to be a male graphic designer in the US?

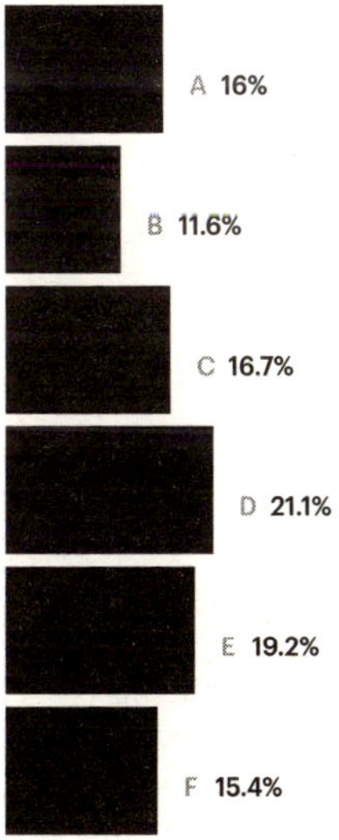

US

= 318 people

Please note that UK / US income brackets, although roughly comparable, are not exactly equivalent.

A £60k+ / $90k+
B £50–60k / $75–90k
C £40–50k / $60–75k
D £30–40k / $45–60k
E £20–30k / $30–45k
F <£20k / <$30k

Gender: UK

What is your annual income before tax?

Paid less than £20k

41%

of women

26%

of men

=
571
people

=
728
people

GD& comments...
These statistics make us feel the industry has a long way to go.

Paid more than £60k

1%

of women

8%

of men

= 571 people

= 728 people

In 2015, the UK government consultation *Closing the Gender Pay Gap* reported that, on average, women earn around 80p for every £1 earned by men. [1]

Gender: US

What is your annual income before tax?

Paid less than $30k

24%

of women

15%

of men

= 302 people

= 318 people

In the US, the gender disparity in earnings was less pronounced than in the UK, but was still definitively there.

Paid more than $90k

9%

of women

16%

of men

= 302 people

= 318 people

In 2013 the Bureau of Labor Statistics report *Women in the Labor Force* stated that the median weekly earnings of US women [working full-time] was 82% of their male counterparts. [2]

Gender

Have you ever spoken publicly about your work [eg giving a lecture, speaking at a conference]?

Had spoken publicly

26%

of women

37%

of men

Of all those who *had* spoken publicly about their work, 65.2% were men.

A
Female
■ 25.9%
■ 74.1%

B
Male
■ 37.3%
■ 62.7%

■ Yes
■ No

=
522
people

=
679
people

Gender

How often would you say you volunteer to speak about your work?

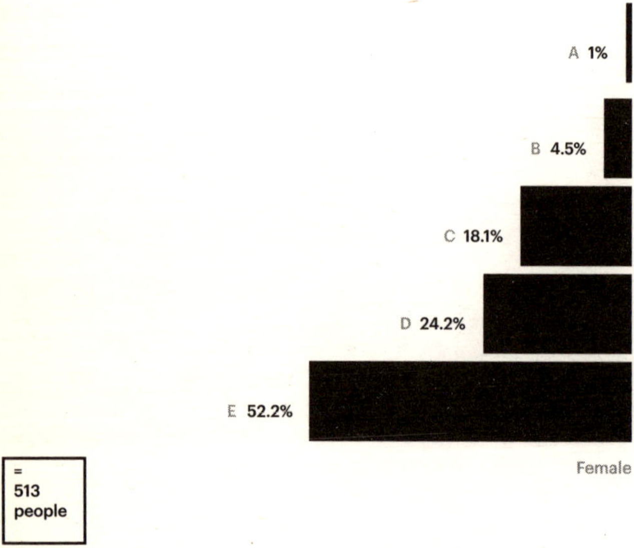

On the whole, men were more likely than women to volunteer to speak publicly about their work.

124–125

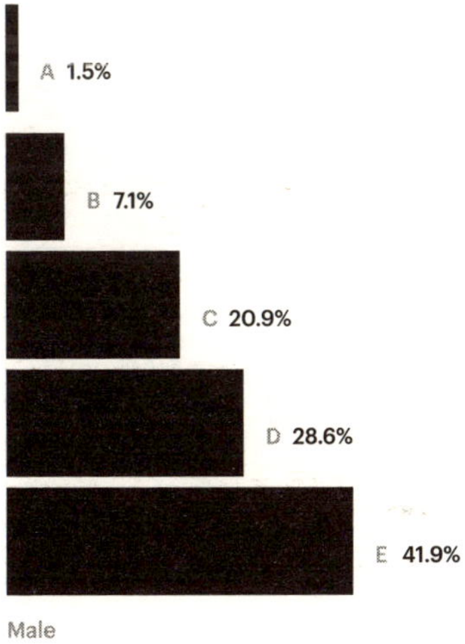

= 664 people

A All the time
B Often
C Sometimes
D Rarely
E Never

Gender

Generally speaking, how comfortable do you feel promoting your work?

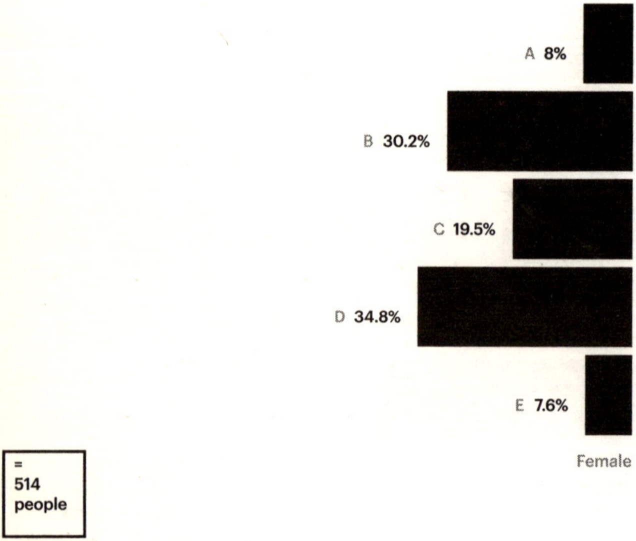

Men reported feeling more comfortable promoting their work than women.

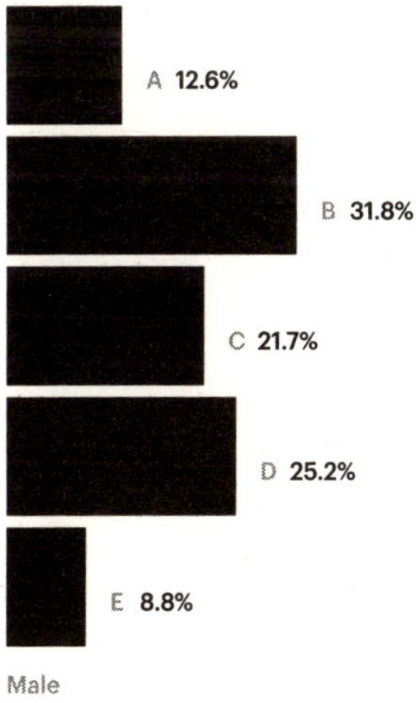

= 674 people

A Very comfortable
B Fairly comfortable
C Neutral
D Fairly uncomfortable
E Very uncomfortable

Gender

Generally speaking, how comfortable do you feel promoting your work?

Very or fairly uncomfortable promoting work

42%

of women

34%

of men

= 514 people

= 674 people

Very comfortable promoting work

8%

of women

13%

of men

= 514 people

= 674 people

Gender

Do you think that the graphic design industry is:

	Female
A feminine culture	2.1%
A masculine culture	47.7%
A gender-neutral culture	44.9%
Don't know	5.2%

= 612 people

Male

1.5%	A feminine culture
28.6%	A masculine culture
63.7%	A gender-neutral culture
6.2%	Don't know

=
727
people

Gender

How do you think your most recent work compares to that of your peers?

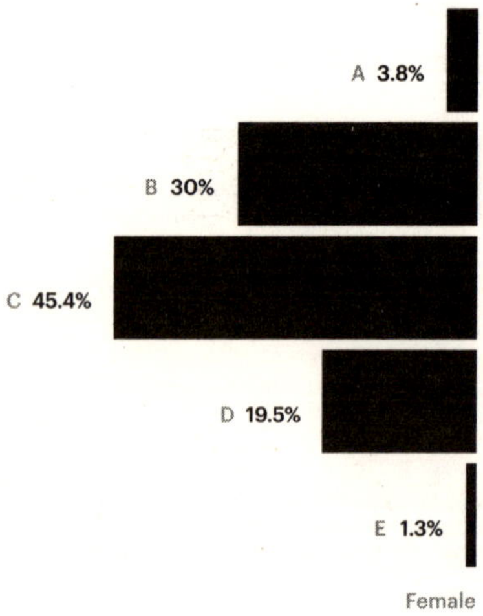

=
601
people

Men were more likely than women to think their work was better than that of their peers.

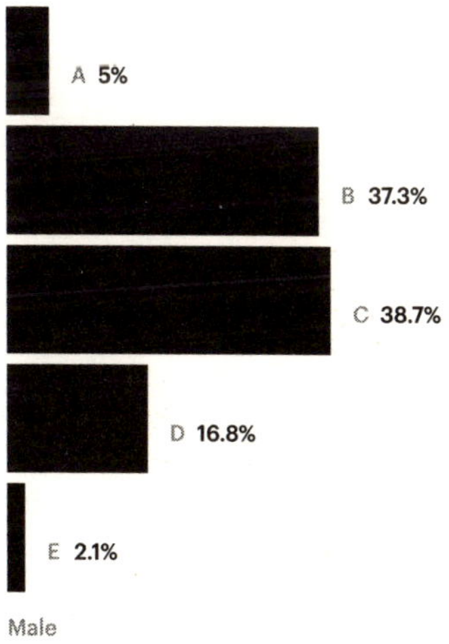

= 715 people

A Substantially better
B Better
C About the same quality
D Not quite as good
E Significantly less good

Gender

All things considered, how satisfied are you with your career?

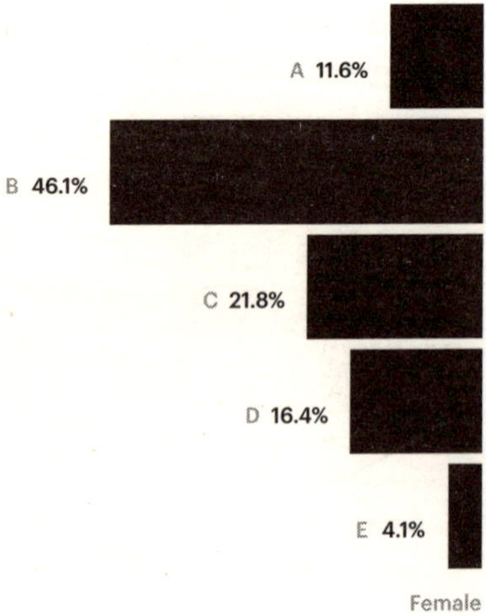

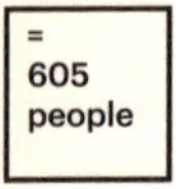

Women were slightly more satisfied with their careers than men.

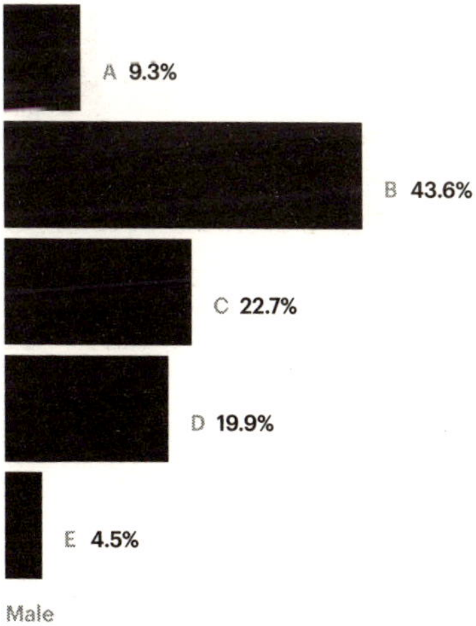

= 718 people

A Very satisfied
B Fairly satisfied
C Neutral
D Fairly unsatisfied
E Very unsatisfied

Gender

All things considered, how satisfied are you with your life?

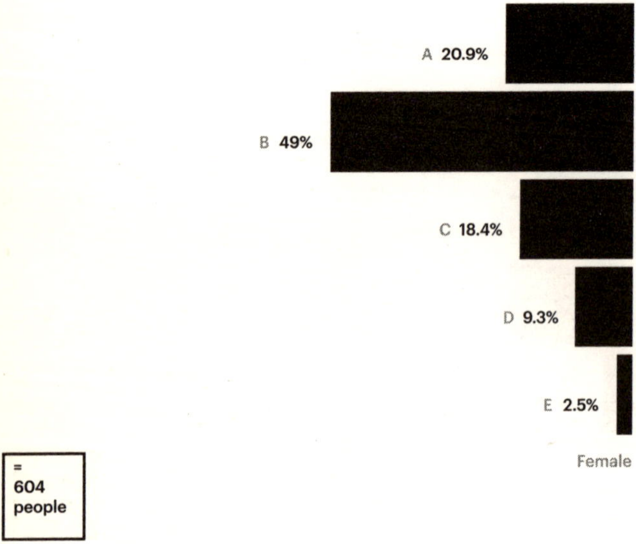

Women were slightly more satisfied with their lives than men.

Respondents reported greater satisfaction with their lives than their careers.

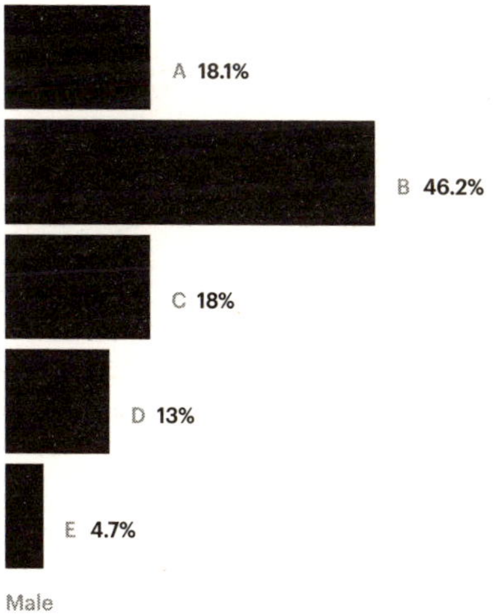

=
717
people

A Very satisfied
B Fairly satisfied
C Neutral
D Fairly unsatisfied
E Very unsatisfied

Gender

Do you keep an archive in the hope of that future retrospective?

Kept an archive

43%

of women

47%

of men

Since its foundation in 1989 the Design Museum in London has never held a major retrospective of the work of a female graphic designer. [3]

A
Female
■ 42.8%
■ 57.2%

= 594 people

B
Male
■ 46.9%
■ 53.1%

= 715 people

■ Yes
■ No

Gender

What do you think most advantages a graphic designer in the advancement of their career?

	Female
Client list	5.7%
Family background in related areas	1.5%
Hard work	34.8%
Talent	17.7%
What they know	5.9%
Which college they went to	1.3%
Who they know	33%

= 609 people

+→ 140–141

Male

4.7%	Client list
1.1%	Family background in related areas
45%	Hard work
18.1%	Talent
5.7%	What they know
1.4%	Which college they went to
24.1%	Who they know

= 725 people

Gender

What do you think most advantages a graphic designer in the advancement of their career?

Men were more likely to think that hard work most advantages graphic designers.

142–143

Women were
more likely to think
that who you know
matters most.

=
1,334
people

Gender: have children under eight

Who is primarily responsible for your child's / children's day-to-day care?

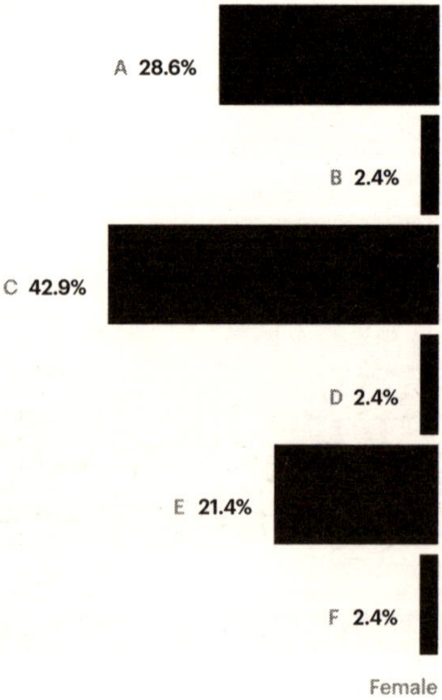

= 42 people

+→ 144–145

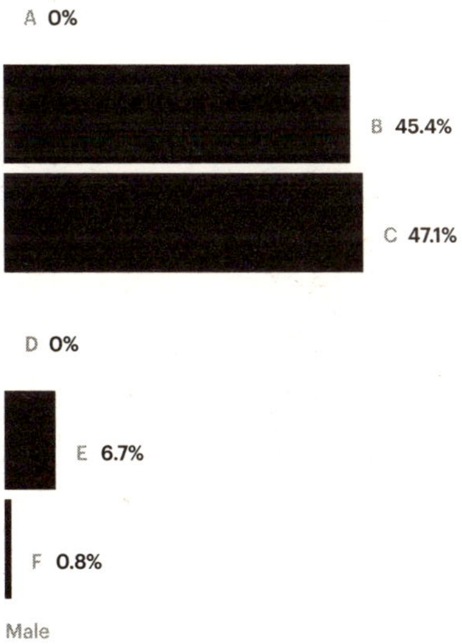

= 119 people

A I am

B My spouse / partner is

C My spouse / partner and I share the responsibility

D A relative or friend is

E A childminder / nanny is

F My child doesn't / children don't live with me

Gender: have children under eight

Who is primarily responsible for your child's / children's day-to-day care?

Both women and men largely shared the care of their children with their partners.

However, 0% of men cared solely for their children, compared with 29% of women.

= 161 people

In 2011 the UK-based Fatherhood Institute reported that, on average, in two-parent families fathers are responsible for 25% of all childcare related activities during the week, rising to one-third at weekends. [4]

Gender: sharing childcare with partner

How satisfied are you with the way childcare tasks are divided?

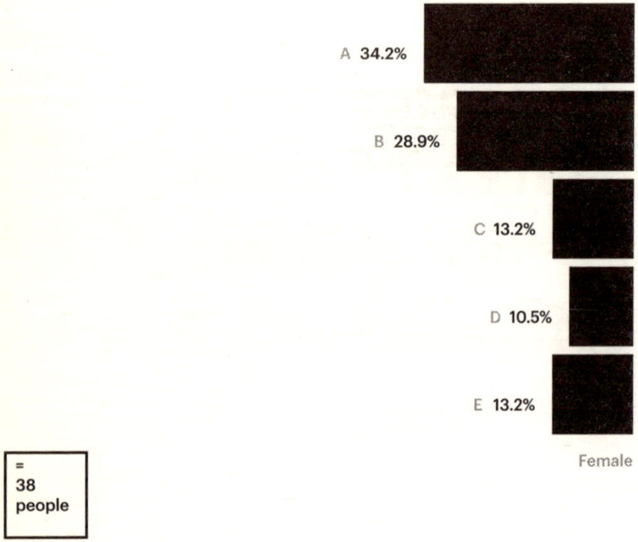

Overall, respondents were satisfied with the division of their childcare tasks, but women were less satisfied than men.

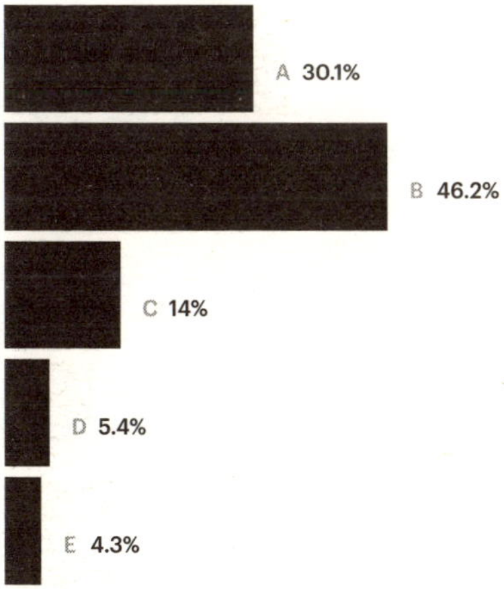

Male

= 93 people

A Very satisfied
B Fairly satisfied
C Neutral
D Fairly unsatisfied
E Very unsatisfied

Education

We were interested in the relationship between education and graphic design. There are many design degree courses – and graduates – across the UK and US, and yet in 2010 the UK Design Council reported that only 51% of practising UK designers actually have a degree. [1] The graphic designers responding to this survey were in fact highly educated – 88% had an undergraduate degree or higher, and 26% had gone on to postgraduate study. Most had studied graphic design specifically, but nearly a quarter had studied a subject other than art and design, confirming our suspicion that graphic design has its fair share of polymaths.

Although relatively small numbers of students and educators answered the survey, their responses help suggest something about the experience of studying and teaching graphic design. Of those still studying, most defined their subject as 'graphic design' at undergraduate level, with 'communication design / visual communication' proportionately more common for postgraduate courses.

an educator. Instead, the main motivations given were teaching / sharing knowledge and shaping the future of the discipline. And it seems that they have plenty of scope, given that so many of our respondents had a graphic design degree.

Education

What are you studying?

Education bubble diagram

Stefanie Posavec, data designer

Of the students responding to the survey, 165 reported both their subject and the level they were studying at. The following bubble diagram shows how those answers break down.

Undergraduate students made up the bulk of the group. While most were studying graphic design or communication design / visual communication, there were a variety of other subjects listed, including advertising, computer science, film design and product design. Most of the postgraduate students were studying subjects closely related to graphic design.

Education bubble diagram

Undergraduate

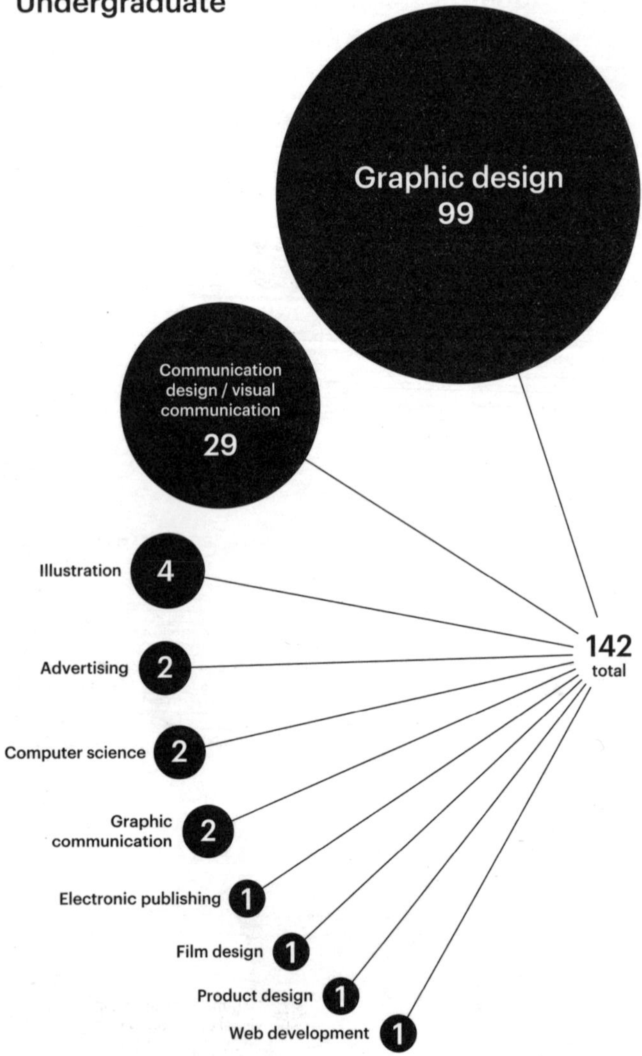

Postgraduate

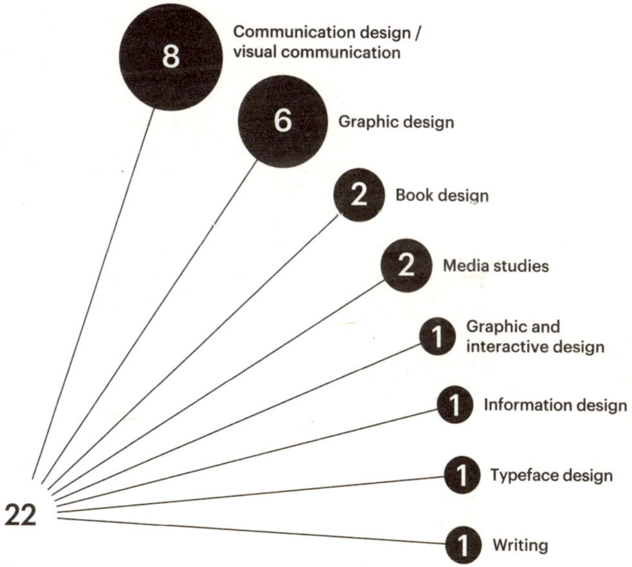

Doctorate

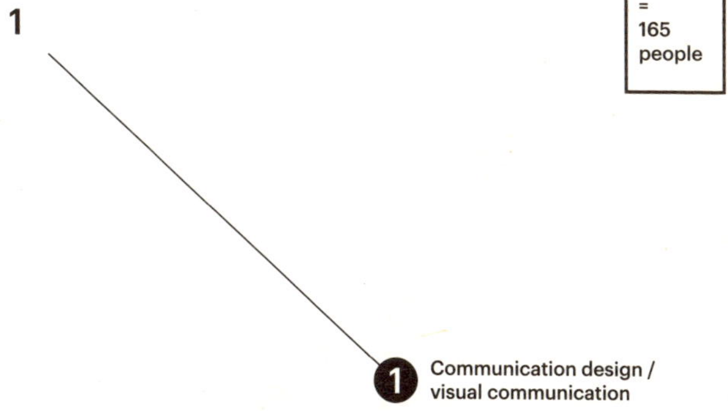

Education

What is the highest level of education you have successfully completed?

88%

undergraduate degree or higher

GD& wonders...
Are graphic designers getting better educated?

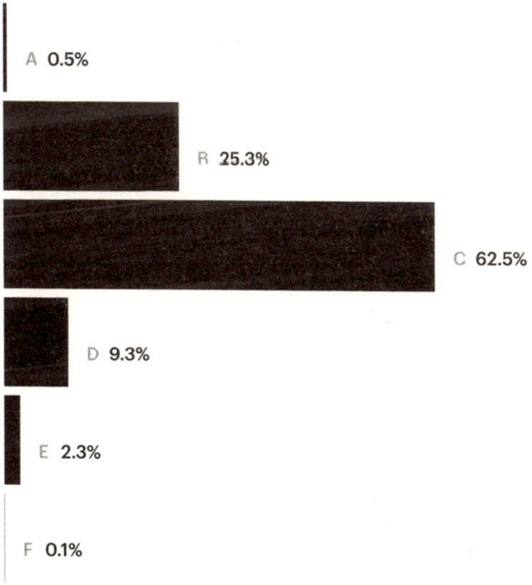

= 1,889 people

In 2010 the UK Design Council found that 51% of designers had a degree or equivalent qualification, which they reported as an increase of 10% from 2003. [2]

A Doctorate

B Postgraduate qualification or degree

C Undergraduate degree

D Further education / community college

E Secondary / high school

F Primary / middle school

Education

To what level did you study graphic design?

81%

undergraduate level or higher

= 1,832 people

Did you study something other than / as well as an art and design subject at degree level or higher?

(←+) 160–161

24%

yes

= 1,883 people

Among those who reported studying a subject other than art and design, these were the three most common subject areas:

30.4%	Humanities
12.8%	Social sciences
11.6%	Engineering / technology

Education: students

What are you studying? At what level?

Across all levels

63%

graphic design

At undergraduate level most students were studying graphic design; proportionately more were studying visual communication / communication design at postgraduate level.

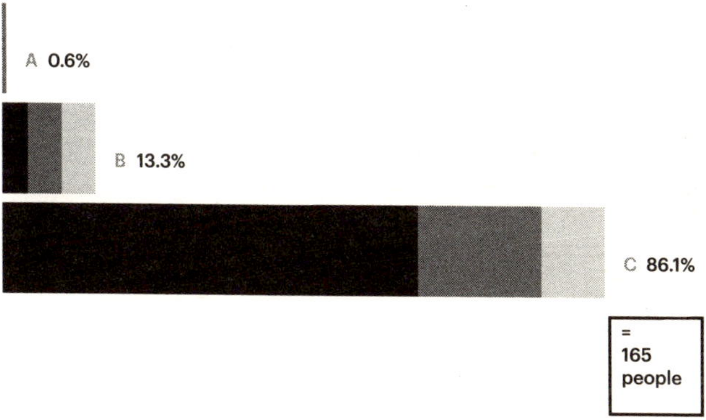

A Doctorate
B Postgraduate
C Undergraduate

■ Graphic design
■ Communication design / visual communication
■ Other

Do you want to become a practising professional in your field of study after you graduate?

84% of students surveyed hoped to continue in their field of study after graduation.

GD& notices...
Of students, 45.3% considered graphic design to be a young person's profession.

Do you think you will become a practising professional in your field of study?

But only 76% of students thought that they would achieve this.

= 166 people

In 2013 *The Washington Post* reported that 27.3% of all US college graduates were employed in a job that related to the subject that they had majored in. [3]

Education: students

What skill do you think it would be most useful for you to develop or acquire?

Students thought networking was the most useful skill they could acquire.

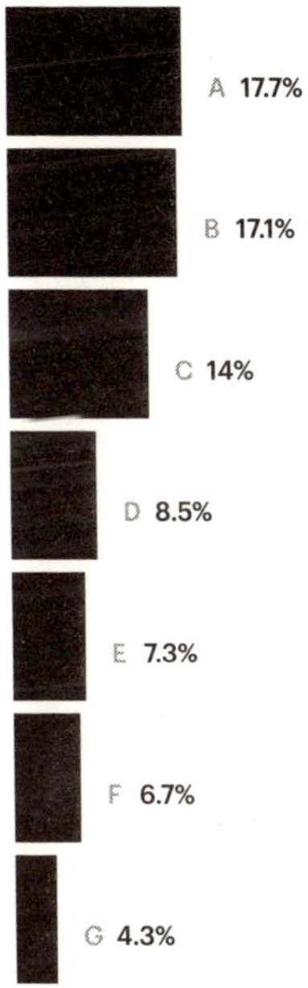

= 164 people

A Networking
B Idea generation
C Programming / coding
D Time management
E Knowledge of the field
F Art direction
G Proficiency at Adobe CS

More responses:

7.3%	Other
3.7%	Presentation skills
3%	Self-promotion
2.4%	Project management
2.4%	Strategy
1.8%	Typography
1.2%	Research
1.2%	Writing
0.6%	Budgeting
0.6%	Image making
0%	Moving image
0%	Preparing work for print

Have you done any teaching in your subject? At what level?

26%

had experience of teaching

= 1,348 people

The Design Council's 2010 report on the design industry as a whole found that 18% of UK design businesses had been involved in design education; only 41% of these were involved directly in teaching. [4]

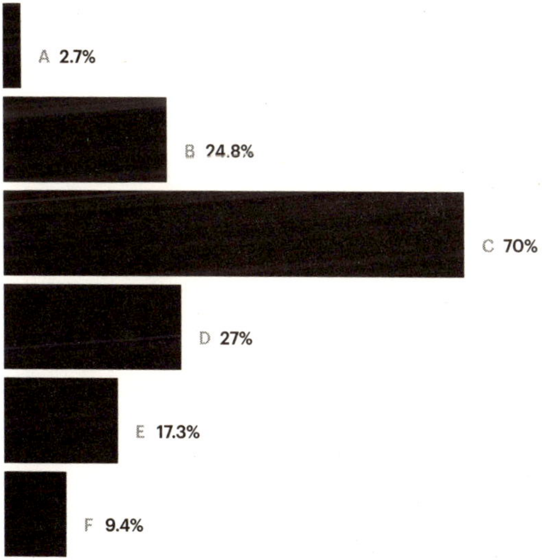

= 330 people

Respondents were asked to specify all levels at which they taught; of the 330 people who answered this question, 35.2% selected multiple answers. For this reason the combined data on this graph equates to more than 100% [each percentage refers to how many of the total taught at this level].

A Doctorate

B Postgraduate qualification or degree

C Undergraduate degree

D Further education / community college

E Secondary / high school

F Primary / middle school

Education: educators

What is the highest level of education you have successfully completed?

89%

of respondents who primarily identified as an educator had a postgraduate degree or higher

= 73 people

GD& notices...
Educators were the most educated group of respondents.

42%

of respondents with some teaching experience had a postgraduate degree or higher

= 351 people

Education: educators

In your current job, what is your primary role?

Teacher	32.4%
Academic / scholar	31%
Course leader	19.7%
Head of department	14.1%
Senior manager	1.4%
Researcher	1.4%

=
71
people

Education: educators

Do you maintain a practice in graphic design or an associated field?

92%

maintained a practice in a related area

This means that only 0.3% of our survey worked exclusively in education.

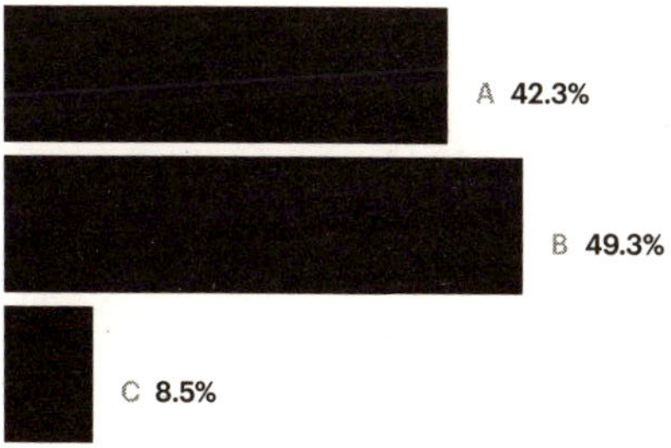

= 71 people

A Yes, regularly
B Yes, from time to time
C No

Education: educators

What was your main motivation for becoming an educator?

45.1% **to teach students /**

22.5% **to influence / shape the future of the discipline**

7% to provide financial security

7% to pursue a research-orientated career

share knowledge

18.3% to keep challenging and developing myself / my practice

= 71 people

1pt = 1%

45.1%	To teach students / share knowledge
22.5%	To influence / shape the future of the discipline
18.3%	To keep challenging and developing myself / my practice
7%	To provide financial security
7%	To pursue a research-orientated career
0%	To influence / challenge industry

Education: educators

What is your annual income before tax?

UK

39%

earned more than £40k

= 44 people

Educators were considerably more likely to earn over £40k / $60k than the overall sample group.

US

62%

earned more than $60k

= 26 people

Education: students

Are you female or male?

60%

female

40%

male

= 171 people

GD& wonders...
Will we be seeing more women in graphic design in years to come?

Are you female or male?

46%

female

54%

male

= 72 people

2011–12 Higher Education Statistics Agency data showed that 61.6% of UK students studying creative arts and design in higher education were female, and that 72.5% of full-time undergraduates at University of the Arts London were female. [5]

Work

A large majority of graphic designers who responded to our survey were working full-time and just over half considered their primary specialism to be graphic design. In fact, most were more than full-time – 78% reported working more hours than they were paid for. Of our respondents, 60% spent more than half of their time designing, with the most common non-design tasks reported as: answering emails [of course], research and going to meetings.

The biggest consensus across the whole survey was that you have to be able to withstand rejection to be successful – it seems that designers need thick skins. This appeared to be borne out by the large number of respondents who were resilient enough to find negative feedback to be 'constructive' or 'an interesting challenge'.

Two skill areas stood out as useful to acquire: coding and self-promotion / networking. The prominence of coding suggests how important online design work has become [62% of respondents had worked directly with programmers].

The desire to improve promotional skills is evident in answers to other questions: designers were confident in their work [80% thought it was as good or better than their peers] but less so when it came to self-promotion [38% were uncomfortable promoting what they do].

While most designers said they would sometimes seek out new opportunities, they were less likely to attend networking events, and would almost never volunteer to speak about their work. However, although only 42% said they were comfortable promoting their work, 45% were quietly keeping an archive for that future retrospective.

Despite most designers being strategic about targeting a specific type of work, and thinking that this is at least sometimes successful, most are not designing what they thought they would be at the start of their careers [see p210]. Winding path or not, it was cheering to see that 83% would recommend graphic design as a career choice.

Work

How long have you been working within design, in years? How old are you?

35%

had worked in design for 10+ years

GD& wonders...
Do designers ever retire?

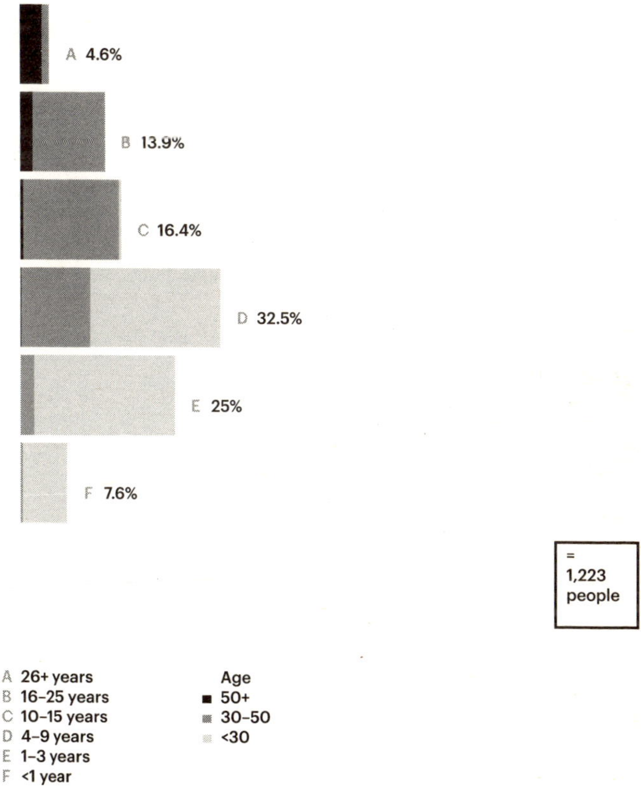
A 4.6%
B 13.9%
C 16.4%
D 32.5%
E 25%
F 7.6%
= 1,223 people
A 26+ years
B 16–25 years
C 10–15 years
D 4–9 years
E 1–3 years
F <1 year
Age
50+
30–50
<30

Work

Which of the following best describes your primary specialism?

51.9% grap de

10% branding

6.6% editorial design

5.7% web design

hic
sign

4.5% art direction

3.5% interaction design

3.7% illustration

3.2% advertising

3.2% typography

= 1,797 people

2pt = 1%

More responses:

3.8%	Other
1.4%	Information design
0.9%	Moving image
0.8%	Type design
0.5%	Animation
0.4%	Programming
0%	Film-making

Do you work part- or full-time overall [even if your work comprises various part-time jobs]?

3%

worked part-time in their main job but full-time overall

60.5% of those respondents working part-time overall were women.

A Full-time
B Part-time

Work

In the past week, were you working predominantly as an employee or were you self-employed / running your own business?

32%

were self-employed / running their own business

GD& notices...
There weren't so many people going it alone as we expected.

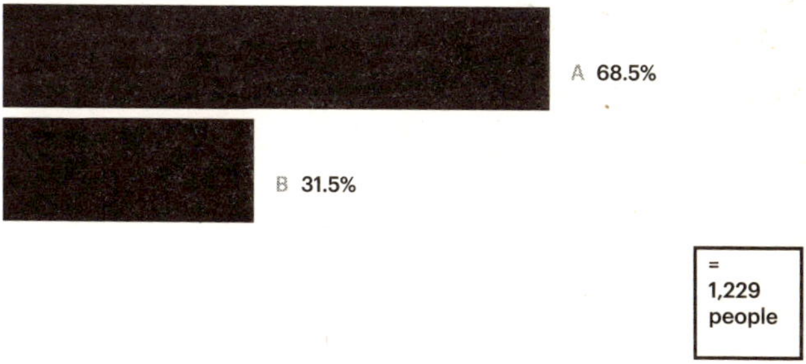

The US and the UK define self-employment differently. Despite this, it is interesting to compare available statistics.

In 2012 it was estimated that 24% of US graphic designers were self-employed. [1] In the UK it was estimated that, in 2010, 28% of all designers were working freelance. [2]

In 2014 the Office for National Statistics reported that 15% of the overall workforce in the UK was self-employed. [3]

A Employee

B Self-employed / running own business

Work

How many people are employed in your main place of work?

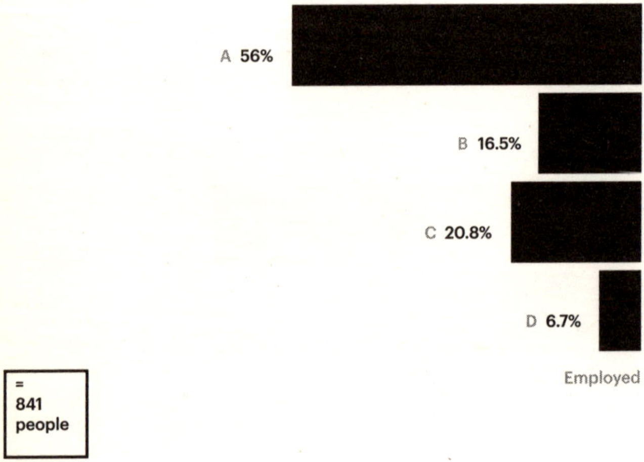

Self-employed / running own business

= 383 people

A 26+
B 11–25
C 4–10
D 1–3

In 2014 the Department for Business, Innovation and Skills reported that there were 5.2 million small businesses in the UK, making up 99.3% of all UK private employer firms. [4]

In 2010 the US Small Business Administration reported 27.9 million small businesses in the US, making up 99.7% of US employer firms. [5]

Work

Generally, how many hours do you work in a week?

58%

more than 40 hours

GD& comments...
Given that 63.1% of our respondents reported being obsessed with their subject, this is hardly surprising.

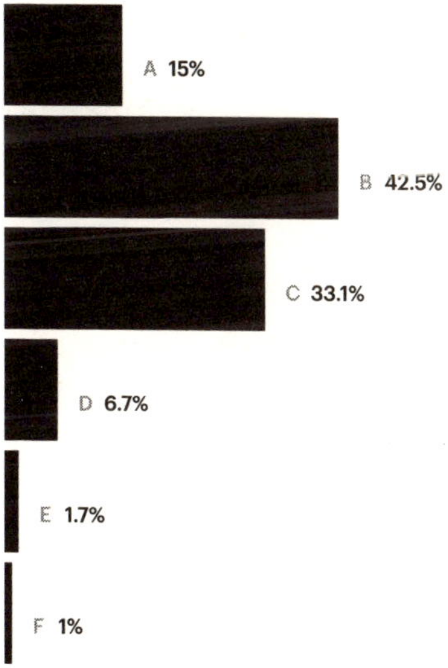

= 1,230 people

A 50+ hours
B 41–50 hours
C 36–40 hours
D 22–35 hours
E 16–21 hours
F <16 hours

Work

Do you work more hours than you are paid to work?

YE

S NO

=
1,344
people

3pt
=
1%

78.1% Yes
21.9% No

Work

Would you prefer to work more or fewer hours than you presently work?

Prefer to work more hours	5.8%
Happy with hours worked	49.9%
Prefer to work fewer hours	44.3%

Of respondents working more than 50 hours a week, 71.3% reported that they would prefer to work fewer hours.

Since 2003, the European Commission Working Time Directive has specified that a working week in the EU must not exceed an average of 48 hours [including overtime]. [6]

Work

Would you prefer to work more or fewer hours than you presently work?

Work 50+ hours per week

Work 41–50 hours per week

Work 36–40 hours per week

Work 22–35 hours per week

Work 16–21 hours per week

Work <16 hours per week

	A	B	C	D
■	71.3%	55.4%	29.1%	8.4%
■	26.5%	43.8%	66.7%	57.8%
■	2.2%	0.8%	4.2%	33.7%
=	181 people	520 people	406 people	83 people

E	F	
4.8%	0%	Prefer to work more hours
38.1%	50%	Happy with hours worked
57.1%	50%	Prefer to work fewer hours
= 21 people	= 12 people	

Are you a member of a trade union or staff association?

8%

members of a trade union

Despite the UK being substantially more unionised than the US, only 6.2% of UK respondents were trade union members, compared with 12.8% of US respondents.

In 2014, 25% of all UK employees [6.4 million] were members of a trade union. [7]

In the US that same year only 11.1% of US employees [14.6 million] were union members. [8]

A Yes
B No

Work

Which of the following best describe your specialisms / primary specialism:

Advertising
Animation
Art direction
Branding
Editorial design
Film-making
Graphic design
Illustration
Information design
Interaction design
Moving image
Programming
Type design
Typography
Web design
Other [please specify]

Specialism relationship map

Stefanie Posavec, data designer

Respondents were asked to give their primary specialism, as well as listing secondary specialisms. With this map, I wanted to highlight which specialisms were most often related. In order to simplify the map, I have only shown relationships where more than 50% of respondents selecting a given primary specialism also selected the same secondary specialism.

Overall, the data confirmed my expectations that natural relationships exist between certain groups of activities.

Work

Specialism relationship map

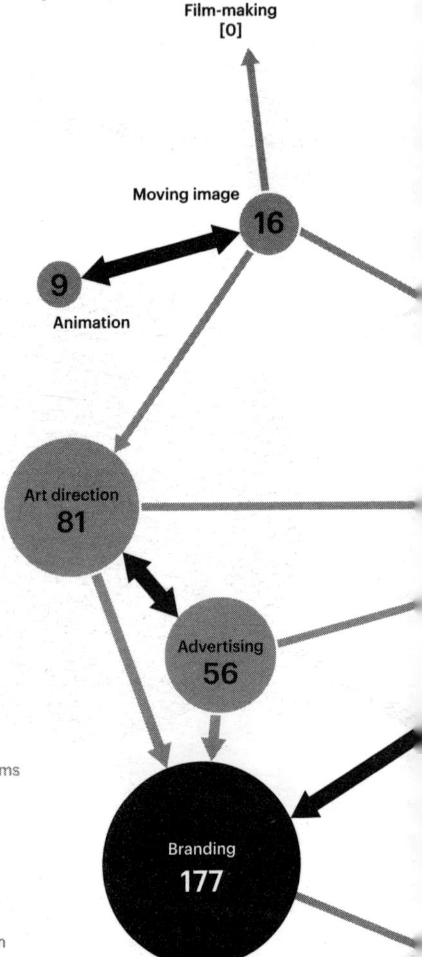

Specialisms

The size of circle represents the number of people selecting this as their **primary** specialism

Black circles pick out the three most common **secondary** specialisms

Relationships

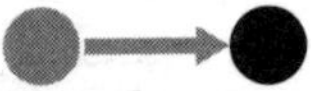

A single arrow points from a primary to a secondary specialism

A double arrow indicates that the relationship between primary and secondary specialisms works in both directions

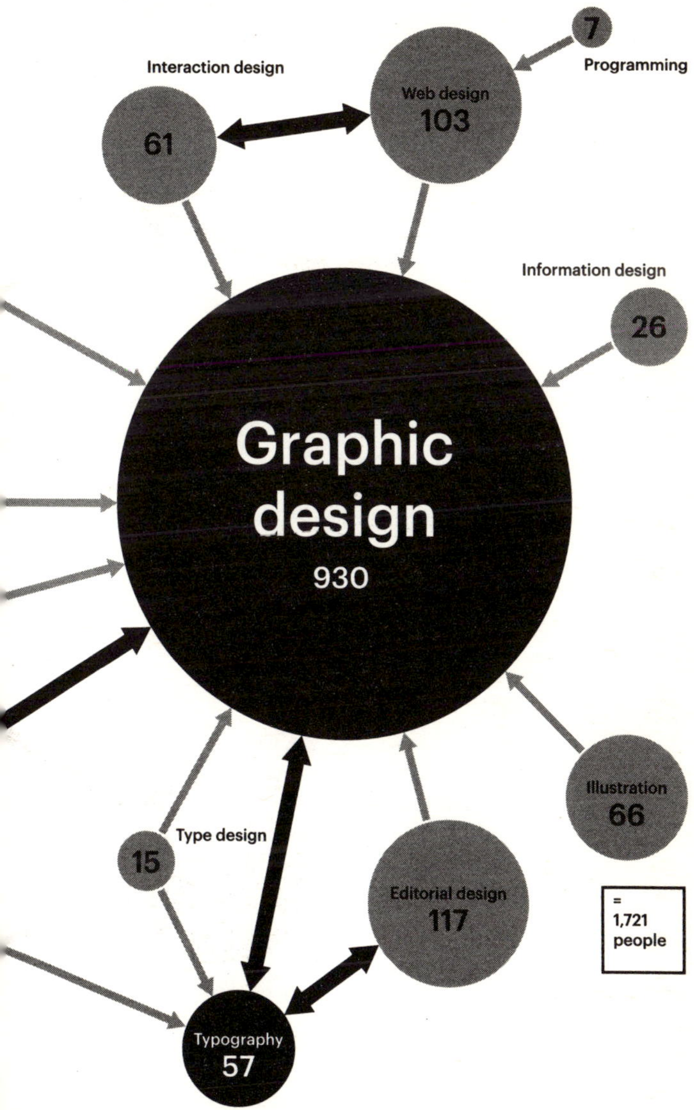

7
Programming
Interaction design
Web design
103
61
Information design
26
Graphic design
930
Illustration
66
Type design
15
Editorial design
117
= 1,721 people
Typography
57

Work

Are you designing what you thought you would be designing when you started your career?

66%

were not designing what they had expected

GD& wonders...

What determines graphic designers' winding paths? Is it changing technology, serendipity or economic forces?

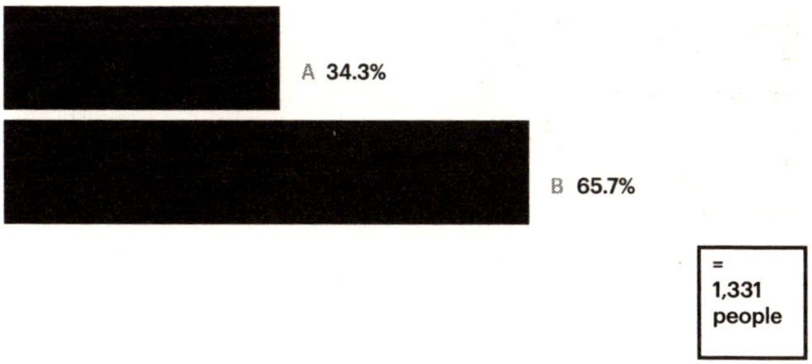

A Yes
B No

As a practising designer, have you been strategic in targeting particular types of work?

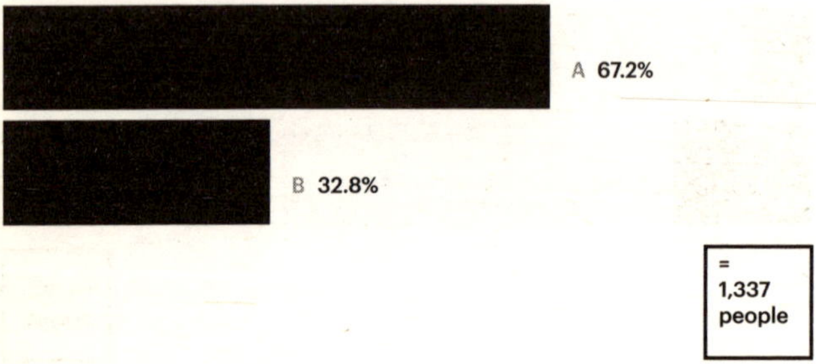

A Yes
B No

If yes, do you think your strategy has been successful?

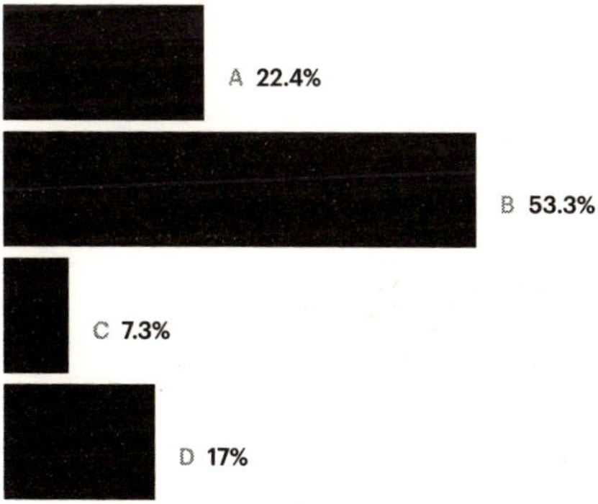

= 1,262 people

A Yes
B Sometimes
C No
D Don't know

Generally, how quickly do you follow up on new contacts?

2%

never

However, 90.2% of respondents had followed up on new contacts after a few days.

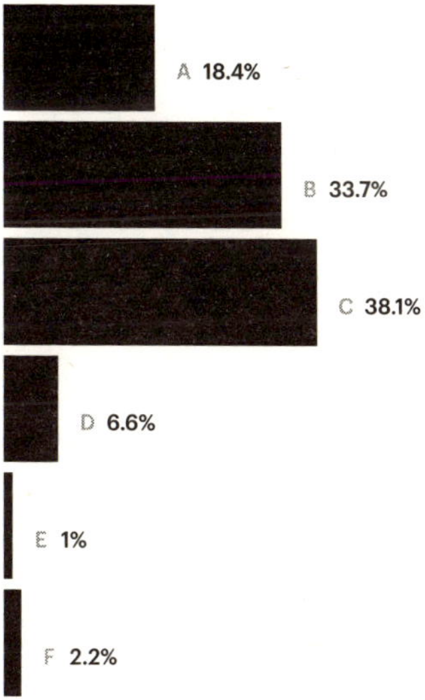

=
1,062
people

A Within a few hours
B The next day
C Within a few days
D Within a few weeks
E Within a few months
F Never

Have you, or the company you work for, ever said 'no' to a job?

78%

had

13%

hadn't, and the rest didn't know

= 1,347 people

Time limitations and financial considerations were given as the main reasons for saying 'no' to a job.

If yes, was the main reason related to:

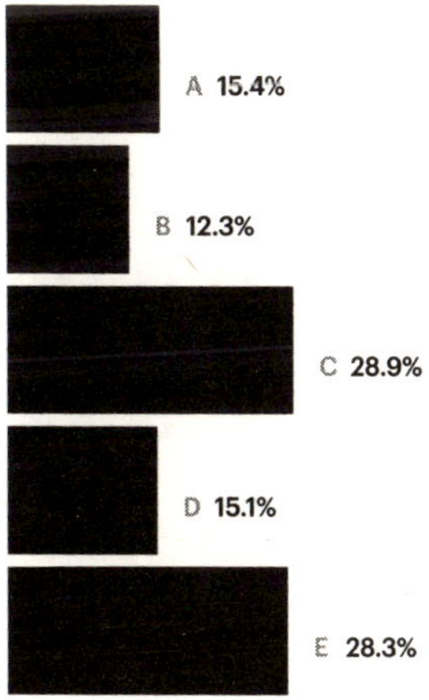

= 1,076 people

A Creative limitations
B Ethical considerations
C Financial considerations
D Poor client relationship
E Time limitations

In a given year, what percentage of your work needs to consist of creatively fulfilling projects for you to feel content?

61% of respondents needed more than half of their projects to be creatively fulfilling to feel content.

9% of respondents needed less than a quarter of projects to be creatively fulfilling to feel content.

= 1,339 people

17.7%	76–100%
42.9%	51–75%
30.5%	25–50%
8.9%	<25%

Have you generally found negative feedback on your work to be:

31.9% con

16.8% dispiriting

13% motivating

3.5% infuriating

3.5% irrelevant

0.8% humiliating

structive

21.6% an interesting challenge

8.9% not an issue

= 1,343 people

2pt = 1%

31.9%	Constructive
21.6%	An interesting challenge
16.8%	Dispiriting
13%	Motivating
8.9%	Not an issue
3.5%	Infuriating
3.5%	Irrelevant
0.8%	Humiliating

Do you think you have to be able to withstand rejection to be successful?

YE

S

DON'T KNOW

NO

=
1,348
people

3pt
=
1%

92.4%	Yes
4%	Don't know
3.6%	No

Work

In a typical working day, approximately how much of your time do you spend designing?

More than half of time spent designing

52%

of self-employed / running own business

65%

of employees

=
377
people

=
782
people

GD& comments...

We thought it would be interesting to see how different modes of employment impacted on time spent designing.

224–225

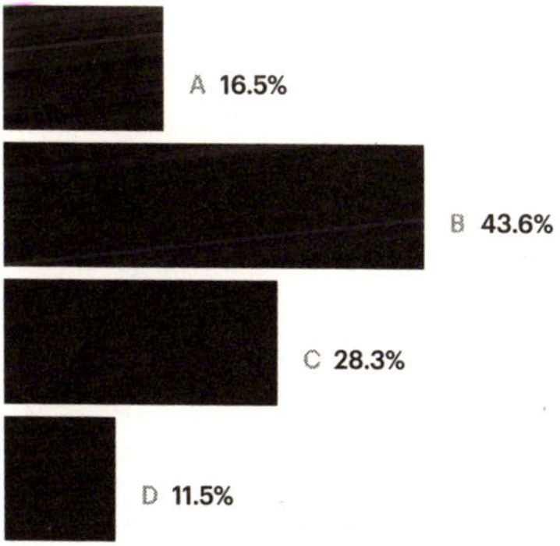

=
1,348
people

A 76–100%
B 51–75%
C 25–50%
D <25%

What are you doing at work when you are not designing?

86%

'answering emails'

= 1,340 people

For this question, respondents were asked to select three answers from a selection of options. This graphic captures 4,456 answers from 1,340 designers.

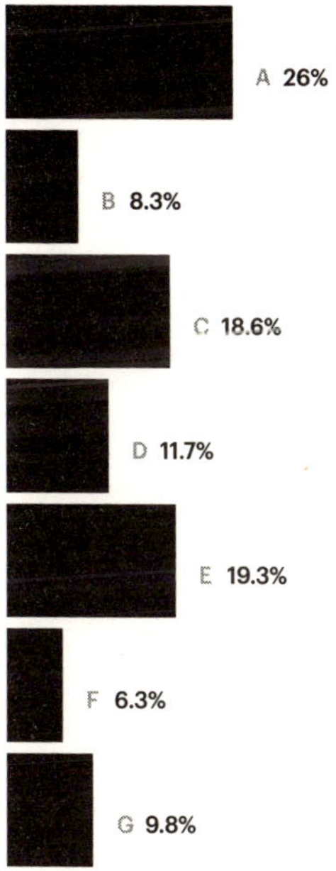

=
4,456
answers

A Answering emails
B Budgeting / scheduling
C Going to meetings
D Keeping up with contemporary art and design
E Project-related research
F Sourcing / liaising with suppliers
G Other

More responses:

5%	PR / communications
3%	Writing tenders / bids / requests for proposals
1.8%	Commissioning

Work

Do you ever get bored by your work?

YE

S NO

=
1,224
people

3pt
=
1%

69.8% Yes
30.2% No

What skill do you think it would be most useful for you to develop or acquire?

11.5% **self-promotion**

6.1% idea generation

6% presentation skills

3.7% writing

3.5% time management

3.4% project management

0.8% preparing work for print

0.7% research

25.4%	Coding	5.3%	Moving image
11.5%	Self-promotion	3.7%	Writing
9.4%	Networking	3.5%	Time management
8.5%	Art direction	3.4%	Project management
6.1%	Idea generation	2.8%	Other
6%	Presentation skills	1.9%	Typography
5.5%	Strategy	1.8%	Budgeting

25.4% coding

9.4% networking

8.5% art direction

5.5% strategy

5.3% moving image

1.9% typography

1.8% budgeting

1.6% knowledge of the field

1.4% proficiency at Adobe CS

0.8% image making

= 1,336 people

2pt = 1%

1.6%	Knowledge of the field
1.4%	Proficiency at Adobe CS
0.8%	Image making
0.8%	Preparing work for print
0.7%	Research

Do you work directly with coders / programmers?

62%

yes

= 1,349 people

Only 10.5% said they could currently code proficiently, but 25.4% thought coding would be the most useful skill they could acquire [see previous page].

Can you code / program?

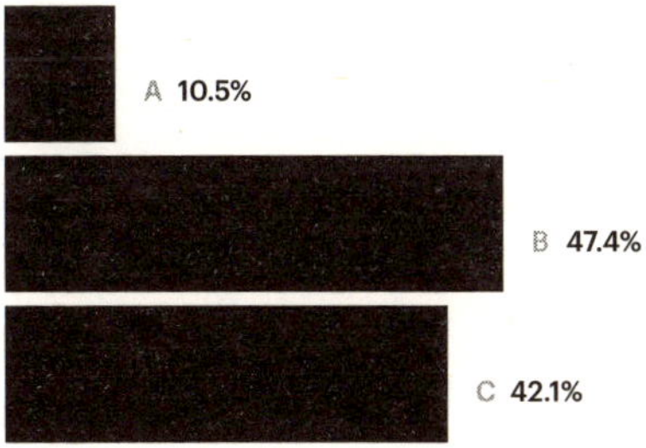

=
1,346
people

A Yes
B A little
C No

Work: business owners

What word would you use to describe your business?

60.6% **st**

11.1% **agency**

7.2% **practice**

5.3% **partnership**

2.4% collective

0.5% _

udio

11.1% company

1% workshop

1% atelier

=
208
people

2pt
=
1%

60.6%	Studio
11.1%	Agency
11.1%	Company
7.2%	Practice
5.3%	Partnership
2.4%	Collective
1%	Workshop
1%	Atelier
0.5%	Foundry

How do you feel about your / your family's financial security?

73% of business owners reported an unpredictable income compared with 45% of all working designers.

Business owners

= 167 people

All working designers

= 1,152 people

What is your annual income before tax?

25% of business owners earned more than £60k / $90k compared with 9% of all working designers.

Business owners	All working designers
= 212 people	= 1,552 people

Do you have interns?

25%

yes

= 210 people

On average, how long have your internships lasted? How long do you expect to be an intern for?

77%

of internships lasted more than a month

59%

intended to intern until they got a job

= 34 people

Work: business owners and interns

What are interns paid?

Salary / wage	76.7%
Expenses	18.6%
Nothing	4.7%

We asked both business owners and interns this question. Of course, interns were only speaking for themselves whereas business owners for their general practice.

= 86 people

The UK and US have different laws regarding interns but, in brief, they will almost always be entitled to all basic employment rights, including minimum wage, which is £5.30 [aged 18–20] / £6.70 [aged 21+] in the UK [9] and $7.25 in the US. [10]

- Business owners
- Interns

Do you know the legal rights of interns?

Business owners

49%

yes

= 179 people

Interns

38%

yes

=
34
people

In the US, there are six criteria that make up the 'test for unpaid interns'; these make clear that an internship is for the benefit of the intern and not the employer. [11]

In the UK, interns can be unpaid only if their internship is a part of their course of study, they are working for a charity / voluntary organisation or they are only shadowing / observing an employee. [12]

Work

Have you ever spoken publicly about your work [eg giving a lecture, speaking at a conference]?

NO

YES

=
1,210
people

3pt
=
1%

67.6% No
32.4% Yes

How often would you say you:
Seek out projects / clients / opportunities?
Attend networking events?
Volunteer to speak about your work?

Respondents were most likely to seek out new projects and least likely to volunteer to speak about their work.

Respondents were asked three questions about self-promotion with the same options as answers. This matrix compares the responses to these three questions. The denser the black, the more people gave that particular answer to that question.

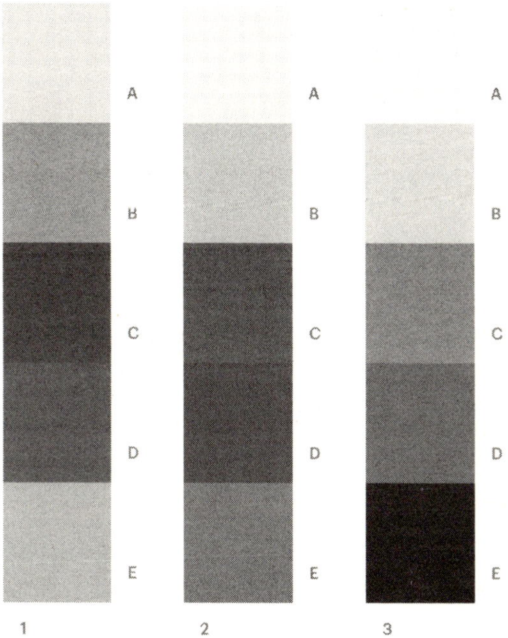

1 Seek out projects / clients / opportunities
2 Attend networking events
3 Volunteer to speak about their work

A All the time
B Often
C Sometimes
D Rarely
E Never

= 1,185 people

Work

Generally speaking, how comfortable do you feel promoting your work?

Very comfortable	10.5%
Fairly comfortable	31.2%
Neutral	20.8%
Fairly uncomfortable	29.3%
Very uncomfortable	8.2%

+→ 248–249

Work

How do you think your most recent work compares to that of your peers?

38%

better than peers

20%

less good than peers

250–251

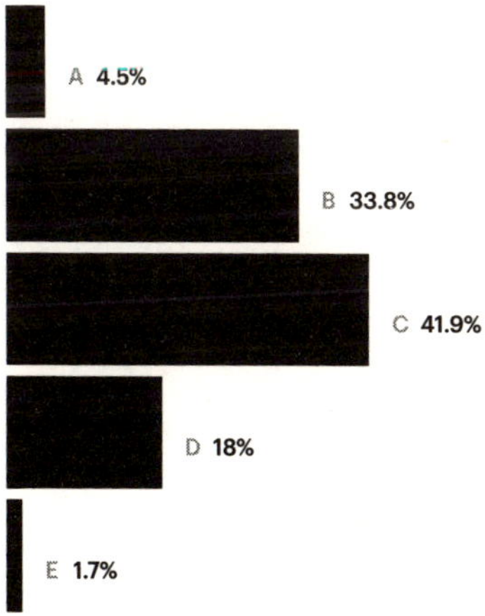

= 1,326 people

A Substantially better
B Better
C About the same quality
D Not quite as good
E Significantly less good

Work

Generally speaking, how comfortable do you feel promoting your work?
How do you think your most recent work compares to that of your peers?

Rather than any particular correlation, this matrix most clearly shows that, in general, people shied away from the extremes.

This matrix shows the relationship between the answers given to these two questions. The denser the black, the more respondents gave that particular combination of answers.

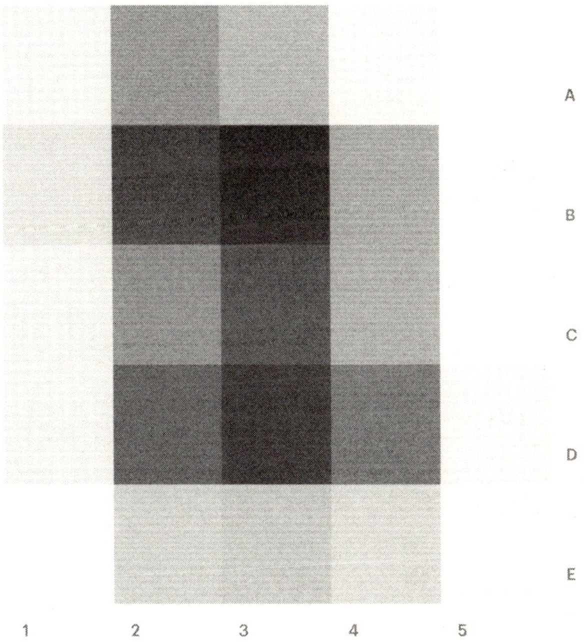

1 **Substantially better**
2 **Better**
3 **About the same quality**
4 **Not quite as good**
5 **Significantly less good**

A **Very comfortable**
B **Fairly comfortable**
C **Neutral**
D **Fairly uncomfortable**
E **Very uncomfortable**

= 1,056 people

Work

Have you or your studio ever won an award or competition?

Total

Had been nominated for an award

Had entered work for an award

Had judged an award

+→ 254–255

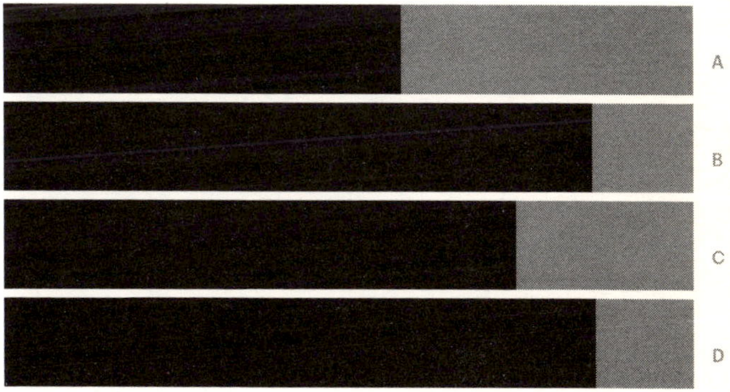

	A	B	C	D	
■	57.8%	85.4%	74.4%	85.8%	■ Had won an award
▒	42.2%	14.6%	25.6%	14.2%	▒ Had not won an award
=	1,190 people	618 people	714 people	127 people	

Work

Have you or your studio ever won an award or competition?

Had entered work for an award once

Had entered work for an award 2–5 times

Had entered work for an award 6–10 times

Had entered work for an award 10+ times

256–257

	A	B	C	D
■ Had won an award	59.3%	78.9%	92.4%	97.9%
▪ Had not won an award	40.7%	21.1%	7.6%	2.1%
	= 108 people	= 389 people	= 79 people	= 96 people

Do you keep an archive in the hope of that future retrospective?

NO

YES

=
1,320
people

3pt
=
1%

In the past decade the Design Museum in London has held six major retrospectives on individual graphic designers. The most recent of these took place in 2011. [13]

55.2% No
44.8% Yes

Work

Have your work-related role models primarily been:

Graphic designers	**56.2%**
Not graphic designers	**31.6%**
I don't have any	**12.2%**

GD& wonders...
Who were the non-graphic design role models?

=
1,344
people

Work

Would you say that you are obsessed with your subject?

YES

NO

=
1,342
people

3pt
=
1%

63.1% Yes
36.9% No

Would you recommend graphic design as a career choice?

83%

said yes!

264–265

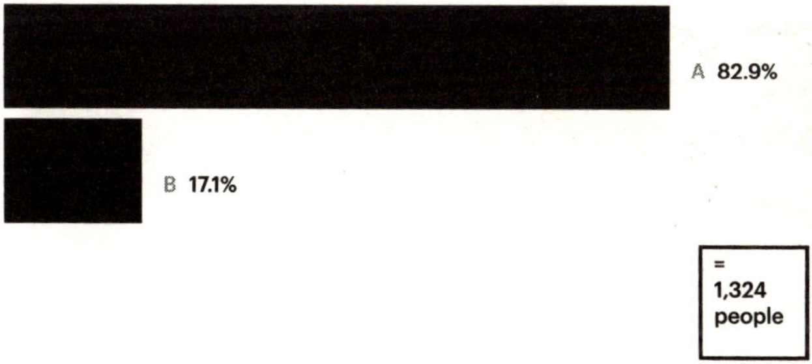

A Yes
B No

Clients

Looking through the Worst / Best section [see p314], you might think that clients are a major downside to being a graphic designer: 16% listed clients as being, or among, the 'worst' things about being a designer, compared with only 3% putting clients in the 'best' column. But the picture that comes through in this section is more complex: 45% of respondents reported feeling positive about active client involvement, compared with only 22% viewing it negatively.

As one might expect, designers are making most of their money through commissioned, rather than self-initiated, work and in most cases it is clients who select designers rather than designers seeking out clients. This obviously has an impact: more than 60% of our respondents thought it was true that their work was only 'as good as the client will let it be'.

Perhaps things could be improved if clients better understood graphic design? Given that 72% of designers adhered to design principles but only 28% thought their clients would understand what that means [see p424] there's certainly a perceived gap. There appears to be an appetite among designers for greater understanding: more than half of respondents thought that it would be good for clients to attend design conferences.

More generally, we were interested to see how many designers were doing work for clients in other countries [61%], that a number never met their clients face-to-face [6%], and that such a substantial proportion of designers' work was pro bono [19%]. And it turns out that at least one cliché of the designer-client relationship is borne out by reality – 90% of respondents had been asked to 'make it bigger'!

Clients

In the past year, approximately what percentage of your work was for the following sectors?

Charities and NGOs	22.1%
Cultural	6.4%
Government	2%
Private business	45.9%
Pro bono	18.8%
Self-initiated	4.8%

GD& comments...
We didn't specify whether the percentage of work should be defined by time, money or output. Sorry!

Respondents were asked to estimate what percentage of their work was done for certain sectors. This graph amalgamates the estimates of 1,138 respondents and expresses them as percentages of the whole.

What proportion of your commercial work is commissioned by clients?

Overwhelmingly, respondents reported making most of their money through client commission.

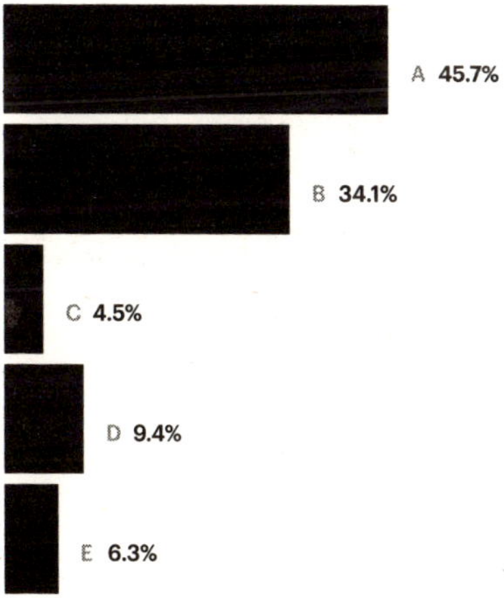

= 1,301 people

A All
B Most
C About 50 / 50
D Some
E None

Clients

In the past year, approximately what percentage of your work has been for foreign-based clients?

11%

more than half

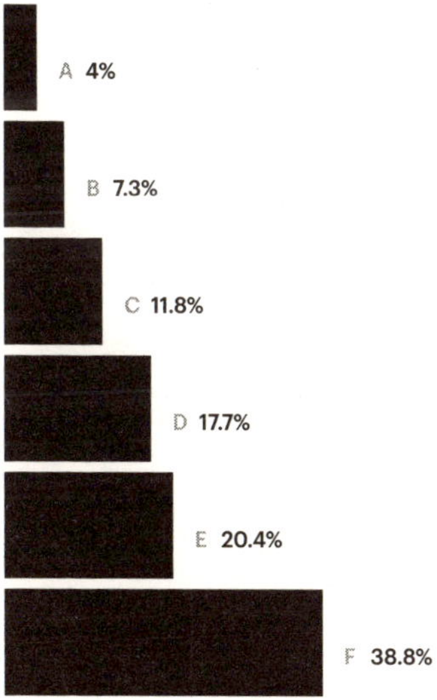

= 1,184 people

In 2013, 8.7% [£17.9 billion] of all UK service exports came from the creative industries. [1] £204 million of this was classified as graphic, product or fashion design.

A 75–100%
B 50–74%
C 26–49%
D 10–25%
E 1–9%
F 0%

Clients

If you work for foreign-based companies, where are they based?

46.3% **North America**

9% South America

6.5% Africa

69.2% Europe

28.5% Asia

11.4% Australia

= 678 people

1pt = 1%

This graphic shows what percentage of respondents reported working for clients based in each region. As people reported working across multiple regions, the combined data in this graphic equates to more than 100% [each percentage refers to how many of the total worked for clients in this region].

Generally speaking, how do you get work?

Clients approached designers much more often than designers approached clients.

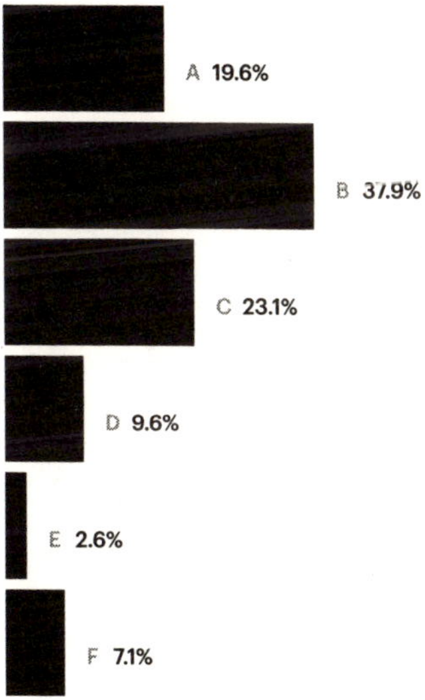

= 1,189 people

A Clients always approach me / studio

B Clients mostly approach me / studio

C Clients approach me / studio and I / we approach them in equal measure

D I / studio mostly approach clients

E I / studio always approach clients

F Don't know

Clients

How regularly do you meet your clients face-to-face?

Often	30.9%
Sometimes	39.4%
Rarely	23.7%
Never	6.1%

GD& wonders...
In a world of Internet technology, is the 'never' percentage going to rise?

=
1,186
people

Clients

How often do your clients take an active role in the design process?

Often	28.5%
Sometimes	54.2%
Rarely	16.4%
Never	0.9%

= 1,190 people

Clients

How do you feel about clients taking an active role in the design process?

Very positive	7%
Positive	37.8%
Ambivalent	33.6%
Negative	19.7%
Very negative	1.8%

=
1,195
people

Clients

How often do your clients take an active role in the design process? How do you feel about clients taking an active role in the design process?

When clients 'sometimes' take an active role in the design process, respondents were generally 'positive' about it.

This matrix shows the relationship between the answers given to these two questions. The denser the black, the more respondents gave that particular combination of answers.

284–285

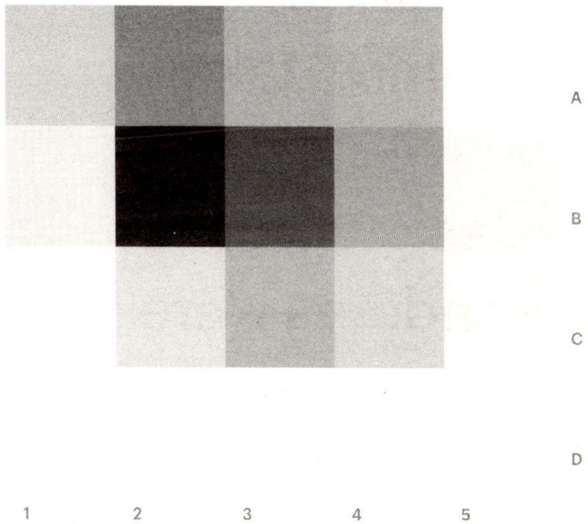

1 Very positive
2 Positive
3 Ambivalent
4 Negative
5 Very negative

A Often
B Sometimes
C Rarely
D Never

= 1,187 people

Clients

Do you think it would be a positive thing if clients attended design conferences?

Yes	52.9%
No	20.7%
Don't know	26.4%

GD& wonders...

Do designers want clients to attend conferences to learn more about design, or so they can meet more potential clients?

=
1,344
people

Clients

In your experience, is it true that your work is only 'as good as your client will let it be'?

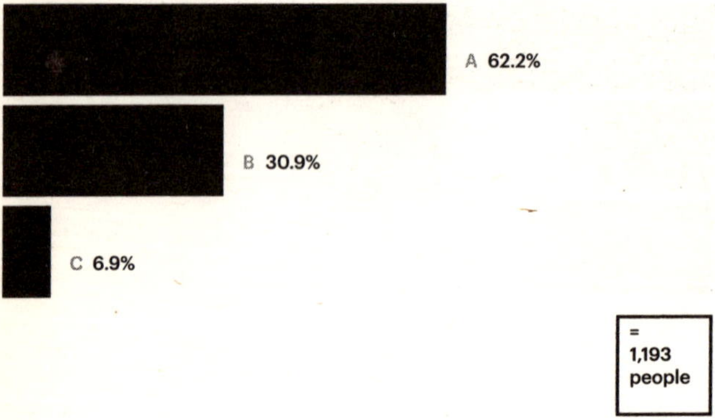

A Yes
B No
C Don't know

Generally, what do you think has the biggest impact on whether clients affect the quality of your work?

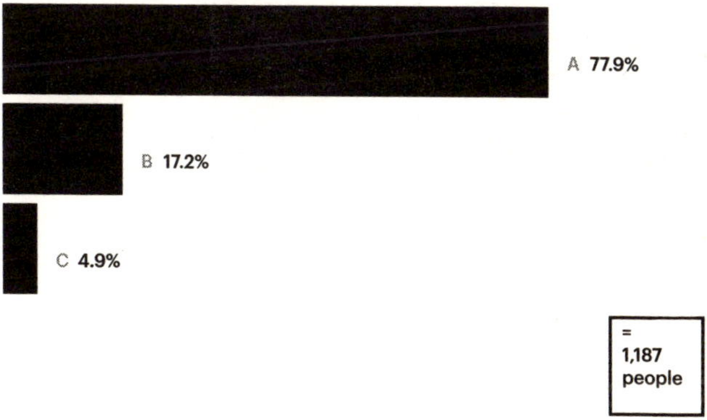

A Specific individuals
B The sector they represent
C Don't know

Clients

Have you ever been asked to 'make it bigger'?

YE

S

NO

=
1,192
people

3pt
=
1%

89.7% Yes
10.3% No

Money

Perhaps more than in any other part of this book, when it came to money we found ourselves wanting comparisons – what do members of other professions earn, what does a graduate from a different subject expect to earn, and which professionals feel most financially secure? However, we found it hard to find directly comparable data.

In the UK, the Office for National Statistics reported that average full-time earnings for graphic designers were £25,507 per year, which is similar to our UK sample group. Other occupations earning at a similar level were tool makers and fitters, retail managers and conference organisers. [1] We also found that the average salaries of our respondents in the UK / US were similar to the overall averages in those countries, but as our sample group is better educated than the average, should they expect to be earning more?

Generally, designers reported that they were 'getting by' or 'living comfortably' on their income but 45% reported that their income was 'unpredictable'. It was notable that those who found the unpredictability difficult were more likely to work longer hours than they were paid for.

Measures of financial security were revealing: levels of home ownership were much lower than the national averages of either country, although this might be as much to do with demographics as designers. [Young urban dwellers have lower levels of home ownership than the national average, and although we didn't specifically ask where designers lived it's likely that many of them are living in cities.]

Overall, financial security was strongly linked to age and tended to be cumulative. Employees were more likely to have pensions, health insurance and income protection. Older designers were more likely to own their homes, and again to have pensions, health insurance and income protection. We wondered if home ownership might be seen as a replacement for a pension, but homeowners were actually more likely to have a pension.

See p072 and p112 for Nikandre's further insights into how living in the UK or US, or being a man or a woman, affects money matters.

Money: working respondents

What is your annual income before tax?

54%

earned £30k / $45k or less

GD& notices...

Taking students and interns out of the equation doesn't rebalance income distribution as much as one might hope.

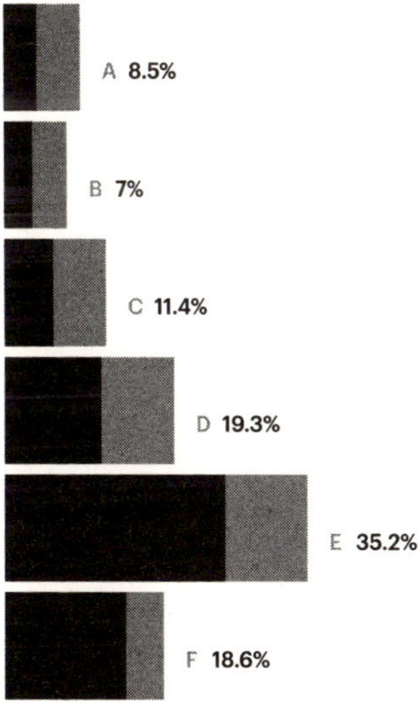

= 1,552 people

	■	■
A	£60k+	$90k+
B	£50–60k	$75–90k
C	£40–50k	$60–75k
D	£30–40k	$45–60k
E	£20–30k	$30–45k
F	<£20k	<$30k

To avoid students and interns skewing the data around money, this section only includes working designers.

Please note that UK / US income brackets, although roughly comparable, are not exactly equivalent.

Money: working respondents

Which of the following best describes how you feel about your / your family's present income?

44%

just getting by

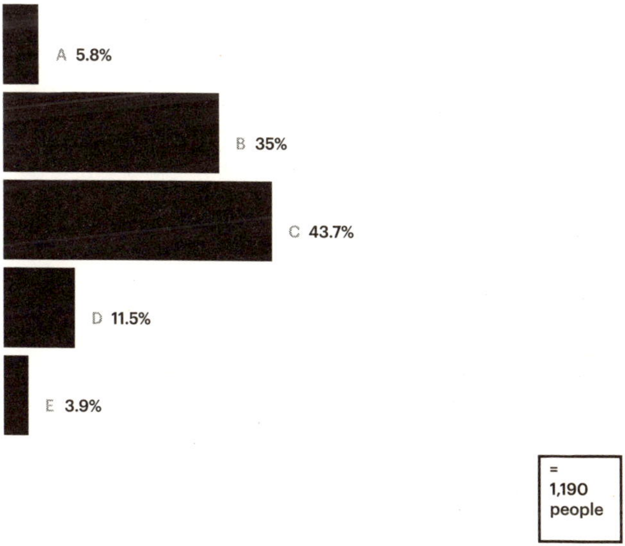

Based on the basic cost of living in the UK, the independently calculated living wage for 2015 was £7.85 per hour, which equates to an annual salary of around £15,500 [based on a 38-hour working week]. [2]

A Living very comfortably on present income

B Living comfortably on present income

C Getting by on present income

D Finding it difficult on present income

E Finding it very difficult on present income

Money: working respondents

Which of the following best describes how you feel about your / your family's financial security?

45%

reported unpredictable income

GD& notices...
That marginally more respondents felt ok about their unpredictable income than found it difficult.

298–299

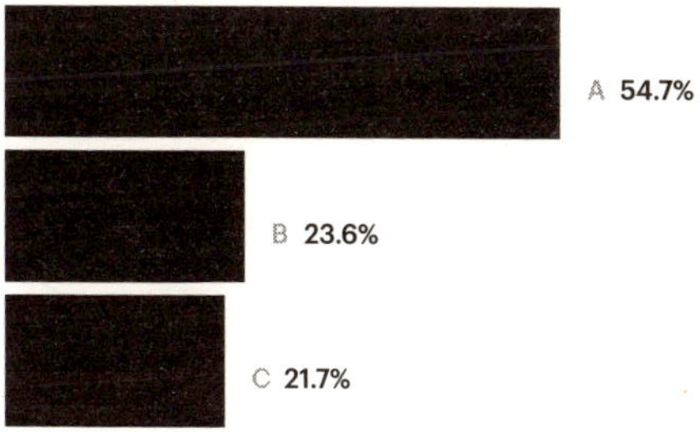

= 1,177 people

A Income is predictable and secure

B Income is unpredictable and I feel ok about this

C Income is unpredictable and I find this difficult

Money: working respondents

Which of the following best describes how you feel about your / your family's financial security?

Worked more hours than paid for

Didn't work more hours than paid for

A	B
■ 51.9%	■ 64.7%
■ 24.7%	■ 24.1%
■ 23.4%	■ 11.2%
= 882 people	= 224 people

- ■ Income is predictable and secure
- ■ Income is unpredictable and I feel ok about this
- ■ Income is unpredictable and I find this difficult

Do you have private health cover / insurance?

Total

UK

US

GD& comments...

It is very marked that the US has a different model of health provision to the UK. We were surprised to see that 19.8% of UK designers reported having private health cover.

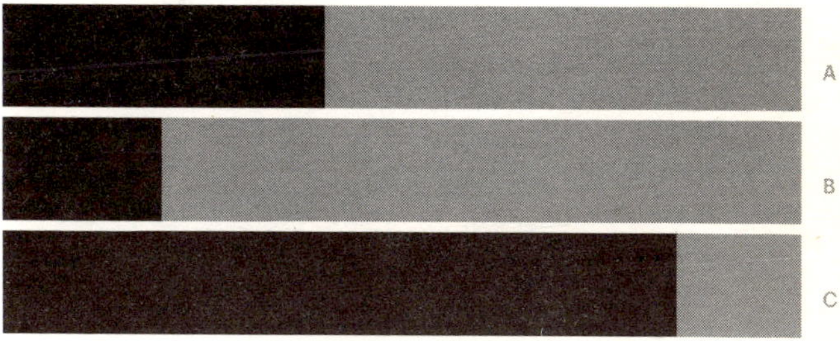

A	B	C	
■ 40.5%	■ 19.8%	■ 84.4%	■ Yes
▒ 59.5%	▒ 80.2%	▒ 15.6%	▒ No

= 1,186 people

= 807 people

= 379 people

Money: working respondents

Do you have a pension / retirement account?

Total

50+

40s

30s

20s

Perhaps unsurprisingly, older designers are more likely to have invested in a pension.

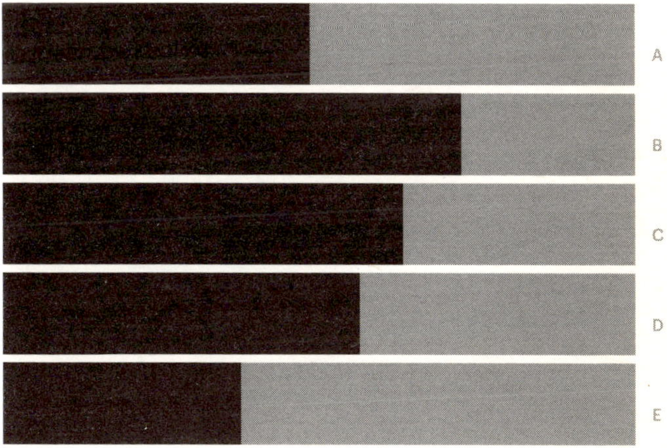

A	B	C	D	E	
■ 48.8%	■ 72.6%	■ 63.4%	■ 56.6%	■ 37.9%	■ Yes
■ 51.2%	■ 27.4%	■ 36.6%	■ 43.4%	■ 62.1%	■ No
= 1,188 people	= 73 people	= 145 people	= 348 people	= 617 people	

Money: working respondents

Do you have income protection / insurance against loss of earnings due to sickness?

Total

Employees

Self-employed / running own business

	A	B	C	
■	25.8%	27.4%	21.4%	Yes
▪	74.2%	72.6%	78.6%	No
	= 1,176 people	= 785 people	= 364 people	

Money: working respondents

Which of the following best describes your housing situation?

10%

rent-free with family

8%

owned by themselves

The number of respondents living rent-free may be related to the relative youth of our sample group.

+→ 308–309

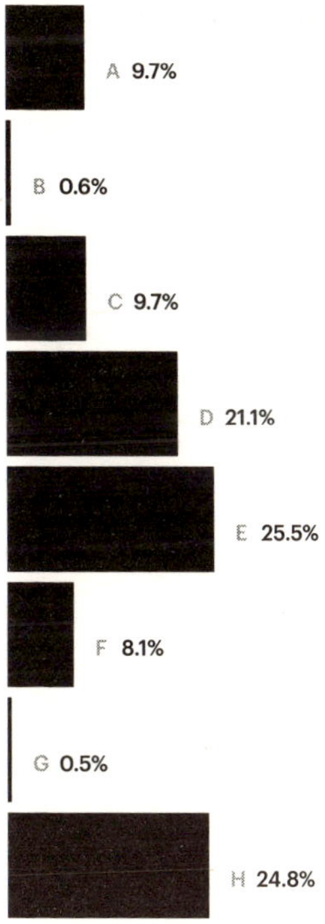

= 1,190 people

A Living rent-free with family
B Living rent-free with friends / others
C Renting on my own
D Renting with friends / others
E Renting with a partner and / or children
F Own by myself
G Own with friends / others
H Own with a partner

Money: working respondents

Which of the following best describes your housing situation?

56%

rented accommodation

Of US respondents, 61.3% were renting compared with 54.1% of UK respondents. Those in the UK were more likely than US respondents to own their home or to live rent-free.

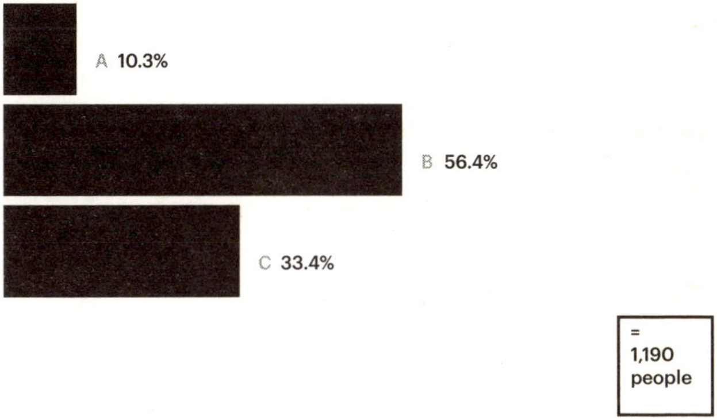

In the 2011 UK Census, 64% of all UK properties were owner-occupied, with the remaining 36% rented. [3]

In 2014 the US Census Bureau also reported a 64% home ownership rate. [4]

A Rent-free
B Rent
C Own

Do you have a pension?

65%

had a pension, compared with

49%

of all working respondents

=	395 people
=	1,188 people

GD& notices...
Home ownership isn't perceived to be a replacement for a pension.

Do you have income protection?

(←+) 312–313

40%

had income protection, compared with

26%

of all working respondents

= 394 people

= 1,176 people

Home ownership, as with other measures of financial security, was strongly linked to age.

Worst / Best

We included a small number of open answers in the survey, despite Nikandre's warnings. She had cautioned that processing data from anything that isn't a multiple choice could be very time-consuming and require a degree of decision-making if the answers weren't clear. However, our nosiness prevailed and we included some anyway – we wanted to capture individual voices and provide space for opinion to be expressed.

The last two questions in the survey were 'what is the worst thing about being a graphic designer?' and 'what is the best thing about being a graphic designer?'; all the responses to these two questions are shown here. Dipping into these pages, readers are offered a quite different perspective on our respondents – a valuable contrast to the graphs and statistics in the rest of the book.

There are recurring themes we might have expected – frustrations with clients, long hours and bad pay set against the joys of creativity and self-expression. But other themes were more surprising. From too much screen-time and bad backs on the negative side, to the variety of experience and getting things out into the world on the positive. We noticed a number of people answering the same for 'worst' and 'best' – capturing a conundrum that a single answer couldn't have shown. Alongside insights into high and lows, lives and livelihoods, commitment and frustration, there were plenty of answers that touched us in their honesty, made us smile and made us think harder about what being a graphic designer really entails.

=
1,128
people

For clarity, minor typographical and grammatical errors have been amended in these answers. We have made every effort to ensure that the essential message has not been affected.

Worst / Best

What is the worst / best thing about being a designer?

Worst	Best
UK respondents	
Not having clients trust your abilities and knowledge	It's constantly changing. Every project is different
	You can choose exactly what you want to do, what direction your career can go in, you can work in all sorts of companies too
Convincing people to trust you	Getting people to trust you
Clients are restrictive	Being paid to be creative
Long hours for no extra pay	I get to do the job I love but just not the right work I would love to be doing
The clients	The work
Always comparing your own work to others and trying to match your [often very high] taste in design	Doing and learning something new every day. Being able to do what you love for a living! The people you meet who bounce ideas off each other, and the kick you get when a good idea comes to life
People always wanting work for free	The variety of work
Timescales and costing; clients not understanding how long a job can take or how much it should cost	Variety of work
Working long hours and for free because you love what you do	Working long hours and for free because you love what you do
Doubting your talent / ability	Producing work that can reflect your own personal style and designing something you can be truly proud of

Worst	Best
Typos	Getting excited when an idea comes together ;)
As a student, uncertainty. In other academic fields your talent / skill is measured by your grades. Gaining a first at uni does not make you a good designer or guarantee a job	For me, the chance to get under the skin of, and learn about, so many different subjects
Being solitary and sitting at computer	Making people look and think
Technical problems	Doing lovely work that helps my clients' success, that pleases them and me and pays me well
Clients' misunderstanding of just how much and how long work takes you	Creating beautiful, problem-solving pieces
When people think it's a profession that only [and ONLY] spends time meddling with Photoshop and the question: 'so you're a designer, can you help me design a logo?'	I believe graphic designers can make a real change in the world
Too much to do, too little time	Seeing a completed project and a happy client [and maybe winning an award for it]
Lack of job security in some instances	Working in the creative industry dosen't seem like having a job as it's something you would do in your free time as a child
It's not well defined yet	The possibility to combine and marry with other disciplines, and the infinite possibilities. The possibility to use it as a tool and not just as a service
Maintaining boundaries between my life and my work	There is a lot of scope for working with others collaboratively. In other creative disciplines this is not always the case
Always believing that THIS is going to be the ONE	Always believing that THIS is going to be the ONE

Worst	Best
Unable to move and exercise, and my eyesight suffering	Creating magic from my imagination
Client liaison as a freelancer is difficult; to balance time and negotiating costs against timing	Relative freedom to develop brand-appropriate solutions
Long hours	Long hours
Spotting bad kerning everywhere and being bothered by it	Being a part of making reality a little bit better-looking
Limitations	Communication
The competitive industry	Being creative
Self-critique	Always looking at the world with new eyes and sharing what you see
Having a sense of humour like none other	Having a sense of humour like none other
Clients art-directing	The ability to constantly develop your style / craft / yourself
Artworking. Clients choosing the most boring option	Great colleagues, those few interesting briefs, being approached by someone who wants to work with you
When other people try to design for you	Creating things and solving problems
Burnout / feeling uninspired	The feeling when you get an idea
Being poor	I appreciate that I am working with different subjects and get to interact with people from different backgrounds
Not being given the chance to explain your work	Feeling part of a club that gets obsessed with type and layout

Worst	Best
Sitting at a computer for long stretches	Seeing your work in use
That you can still get pigeon-holed	That you are creative enough and resourceful enough to break out of the pigeonhole
You are rarely given credit for the work you do when working in a company – your boss / superior who meets with the client will take the credit	The job
Last-minute work. Someone always 'forgets' an event ['it's in two days, can you just...?'] so you have to drop everything to solve someone else's poor planning	Seeing finished work completed and a happy client. Plus when they pay on time!!
People not taking my career seriously	Getting paid for doing something I love
Corporate companies	Being creative
People thinking they know better than you	Being creative and not feeling like my job is a job
Being obsessed with fonts	Being obsessed with fonts
When someone superior to me has their opinions on design and we have to somehow cater to their requests	Always being able to freelance as a backup
	Creativity
Long hours	Seeing your work in situ
It's competitive and sometimes diluted by too many job titles and people	Working in the creative industry is fun and inspiring as there is always lots to see, read and learn. The work and clients are always so diverse
Unsociable hours	Camaraderie
Sitting in front of a screen all day	Seeing your work out in the world

Worst	Best
Sometimes you are not doing the best design work because of what the client wants, it is not always interesting and challenging	It is an ever-expanding discipline and has no real creative restrictions as to the industries you can get involved in
Clients' lack of knowledge of how much work goes into producing designs	Creative freedom
Trying to get your name out there after graduation / during uni	Meeting other designers and being able to bounce ideas and get inspired
The clients	The buzz
Client feedback	Variation of work
Being sat behind a screen for too long... lack of movement and artificial light	
People not understanding what our job involves, and as a result thinking our job is easy	Helping people solve their design problems
The pay	The work
Everyone getting to have an opinion and influence work in progress	Seeing your work in the real world and in people's houses
Clients viewing you as a Mac worker for their ideas that Microsoft Word doesn't allow them to do	Providing clients with a solution that they feel meets their needs and is visual, impactful and well-designed. Then having that work seen
That people expect you to do things for free / cheap just because you enjoy it	Seeing a client's reaction to something they really love and which has exceeded all their expectations
Comparing yourself to others	To connect with an audience your way
Clients who think they are graphic designers themselves	Being creative and having an in-depth knowledge of the different areas of Adobe CS compared with my marketing team

Worst	Best
Finding motivation	Being creative
People misunderstanding you – I always find clients misunderstand me or some of my design choices	I'm a print designer so seeing my finished book or print-based media designed is a highlight for me, as well as smelling it
Long, unsociable hours in busy design agencies. Requests for Comic Sans, 12pt body copy and clip art from clients. At the moment, being made redundant after local government has outsourced work in cost-saving exercises	Open briefs with control of layout, images and typography, working with a client who understands free space and expressive images
Being asked, 'can you jazz it up a bit?' and being expected to work for free	Working in a job I love / live
Misunderstanding, and people asking for free stuff all the time	Being able to think out of the box and get inspired by people – and inspire others as well
Irregularity of work, long hours, not being able to switch off	Creative integrity and freedom
People not understanding how you can get work as a designer, such as asking 'but what does a graphic designer do?'	We're one of a kind, the best thinkers
Trying to find work and having to work for free	Being able to notice and appreciate the small things in life
People not respecting art and design at university level	Beginning to design in ways that could shape the way in which we live. The excitement most creatives have for working with other designers
Under-appreciation from others about the subject of design – it is often an undervalued skill	You see the world in a different way, and creating great, functional work is very rewarding
Xmas cards / material	Being creative and using your imagination

Worst	Best
The saturated job market	Seeing your work out in the world and being appreciated
Clients	The ability to work for yourself on projects you enjoy
People looking down at your career / educational choices because they view design as something unintellectual	I get to do the thing I love all the time and be surrounded by things that interest me. I feel like I'm cheating in some way because I genuinely love what I do and that seems to be rare among people I know
Others not really understanding what you do	Creating beautiful things that you're really proud of
Being overly sensitive	Creativity – the adrenaline rush
	Doing something you love
The sometimes dull projects, and the little respect from other departments	Being creative
Creative block	The thrill from exciting ideas
It's not understood by many as a skill	Having the freedom to think creatively and act on it
Doing things that you really don't want to do, also making things bigger and people not trusting your opinion as a designer	Getting to create wonderful artwork and seeing it printed or online and thinking, 'I've done that'
Co-workers who aren't designers, who tell you how to design things	That I'm not unemployed, having spent £22k on an arts degree
Not having enough time outside work for other things	Recognition for work. Seeing a happy client. Seeing good work being used properly by clients
To be expected to live, breathe and be your job	To be able to make the world more beautiful and easier, even if just a little bit

Worst	Best
You need time to get to a good salary	Challenges every single day and so much to learn – there's always an opportunity to go off on a different tangent within design
Having to educate and hand-hold some clients unfamiliar with the design process	Being creative, and the excuse to try new and weird things in the name of 'process'
Not the greatest pay, subjectively	Having a fun job
Struggling with the new talents that come through from universities every year. Keeping a creative spirit in a corporate position	Thinking creatively, doing something that impacts on people
Boring projects and overbearing clients	Being able to do what I like as a career
Stupid clients having too much say	Creativity and freedom
Constantly analysing, creative pressure	Visual pleasure, detail-focused / observant, informs / influences all other fields of interest [photography, architecture, fashion, illustration, art]
Everyone has an opinion about design and people often think theirs is as valid as a trained designer. It's hard to exert your design authority / expertise	Constantly learning / being challenged as a result of applying creativity to different subject matter
Adhering to clients' bad taste	Getting to do what I love every day
The hours and lack of respect – 'everyone can be a graphic designer' – yeah, right	Being surrounded by beautiful, interesting things. You can make your own Christmas cards. Flexible hours
Time balance	It's what I am passionate about
People assuming you can draw	Getting to play around with images and type for a job
Long hours	Making nice work

Worst	Best
Having to design things the client dictates	Being creative every day
Having creative block	Working with interesting projects
Having to compromise	Making new things
Not being able to switch off	Not being able to switch off
Spending too much time in my office job and not having enough time to work on personal projects I am inspired by or networking with fellow creatives	Having fun and getting paid for it, being exposed to other people's ideas and seeing yours come to life in the real world
1 The hierarchy in workplaces is incredibly unmotivating 2 That you often end up doing 'slave-design', where someone is telling you how they want things to look, without you having to be a part of the creative thought process	When you finally get to do that one creative piece of design from start to finish and you have time to be creative with it
No one knows what you really do but everyone seems to be doing it	Creativity
Deadlines and time pressures	Everyday creativity
Lots of opinions that don't match from clients, and conflicting feedback	Creating and working with others
Working with people who don't respect design as a profession	Getting a print delivery of something you're proud of
Being creatively restricted by clients	The variety of interesting projects you get to work on
Not having the time / energy for my own projects :(	Constant creativity and a sense of accomplishment
Clients who say, 'I'll leave this completely up to you' and then hate the result	Playing around in CS all day like a kid with finger paint, and getting paid for it

Worst	Best
I find it most difficult when a client wants the work to suit their personal taste without consideration of their audience	Exploring different subjects to understand how to solve a problem
Always having to compromise with everyone to get sign-off	Getting paid for making things look nice
Money	Working with curators, writers, designers, architects… learning every day
Not being used to my full potential	Feeling proud of my work
Agonising that you / your work aren't, and will never be, good enough	The very momentary satisfaction in something you've created
Working nine days a week and not working face-to-face with people	Solving problems successfully
Big-headed idiots in the industry	The feeling when you love your finished product
Lack of respect for your craft / knowledge	The type of projects you get to work on
Staring at a screen all day, sitting still all day, missing the sunshine. And spending time on the smallest parts of a project that seem so important during the day – when actually it is the most unimportant thing you could possibly do in relation to the rest of the world. Walking out at lunchtime in the fresh air gives you this perspective. Also the stress – it's quite a stressful job, and not really having any creative freedom, you are sometimes put behind bars by the client. I miss the physicality of the work. When I was at uni you designed and made something and could hold it in your hand and appreciate the good job you did. Now, it just disappears into cyberspace in a PDF nowhere near as impressive. I miss making things	Being creative for a job, but I think this is so diluted now. I love the atmosphere in London, meeting people, going to exhibitions, talks and being inspired at every opportunity. It motivates me and really pushes me to make great work. But being back on a Monday morning, sat in front of a computer in the same spot I always sit, completely strips that inspiration from me and I lack any sort of energy for creating

Worst	Best
The majority of clients are fearful of real change or something new, so you will often end up designing the same thing over and over	I get to work in an industry in which I have a personal interest, and with people who appreciate design
Design by committee or mismatched ideals between team members on a project	Job satisfaction when a client is pleased / proud of the end result
Expensive equipment. Low pay for hard work	Meeting other designers. Knowing how to make things, and the 'successful project' feeling
Currently for me, the company I work for is poorly structured and account management is pretty much non-existent so the worst thing is no project management, ruling by fear and general abuse and treatment like you're an idiot for not having all the info required [when it was never provided]	Being allowed to create things all day
Being paid less than you're worth due to your age	Getting to thrive in a creative environment every day
Long hours and having to work mainly on a computer	Meetings lots of interesting people. Being able to research a subject. Creativity
Emotions. You need to have a big heart but know how to not get hurt, as it requires / involves a humanistic approach	Being creative and using it for a huge audience
Having to design something to someone else's styles and standards, and not your own	Spending time on a project that is enjoyable and results in being able to hold or see that final product that other people can enjoy or benefit from
The subjectiveness of non-design people's views on design	The variety of jobs and clients
Working with clients who think they can design better than you	Making great work that makes a difference

Worst	Best
Lack of appreciation	You can do what you want
Questions like, 'what is your favourite Pantone colour?'	Being able to stay curious
Expensive software	Being creative
Bad designers, who think they are good designers, who create bad stereotypes [but this also creates an advantage for good designers]	Everything. Loving what you do and helping people with the creative skills they need. Complementing people with different skills and working in teams. Critical thinking and not being precious about work, but functional. I love what I do and I always will. It doesn't matter what type of job I receive, as long as it stays interesting and everyone puts their heart to it. Being surrounded by great people [designers and non-designers] and motivating each other
Stinging eyes. Too much screen time	Collaborative. Working with smart, sensitive people. The joy of colour
The expectation to do 'actual design work' [aka glued to the screen] most of the time and not having inspirational events such as art gallery visits or conference attendance included in working hours	Creating work from scratch and crafting
Do what you love, love what you do	Do what you love, love what you do
Jobs you do for money rather than love	Doing jobs for love
Being sat at a computer all day in my current job	Freedom to explore
When looking for a new job and being told as a designer I have to have HTML, CSS, etc too... Stop trying to lump these jobs together. I can design for web, I can't then code it for you too	It makes you look at the world differently

Worst	Best
Worrying whether I'm good enough / not feeling good enough	Getting to create things every day
My work is never good enough to me	Working creatively
Fussy clients with bad taste	Being creative
Constriction of budget and clients who feel they are designers	A client who trusts you to do your job but challenges you to push your limits further
Competition and getting work	It's satisfying being able to express your ideas through important pieces of graphic design, which people will find useful yet will appreciate
Self-doubt and constantly worrying you're not good enough or won't get that 'dream' job	The variety and excitement of brainstorming and concepting a project in the early design stage
	Freedom
The feeling of insecurity about not doing a 'good job' and making quality work in time for the deadline	The satisfaction and enjoyment that comes with communicating with, and to, people
Deadlines	Completing a project
That it feels like the skill isn't taken seriously by most people / clients – people seem to talk as though how it looks is as important as the content, etc and therefore it should be cheap and look the way they had it in their heads before they asked you to design it	That it is a fun job most of the time, and pretty loose
Long, unpredictable hours, unpredictable income, long hours sitting down	Being able to express your aesthetics, being able to create, having an appreciation for beautifully designed things, flexibility on holidays [when freelancing], working on a different project every week
Being asked your favourite Pantone colour	

Worst	Best
Not being able to stop until I'm happy with a project = working lots at home	Work is fun
Being undervalued, and clients don't trust us	It can be interesting work, it's mobile
It is never finished	Being paid for my hobby
Long hours	I get to look at beautiful things every day and get paid to do be creative doing this thing I love
Never leaving the work at work	Never leaving the work at work
Talent	Making everything looking great
Self-doubt	Creative outlet
Arrogance	Prestige
That fine art takes the higher ground	Freedom to roam across disciplines and subjects
	Frequently meeting different people and engaging with different subjects and content
Lots of work, becoming tired	Pay, and joy of creating a masterpiece for clients
Working in a corporate studio that doesn't try to innovate and gives solutions that were old and used, even in the 80s	Being able to build your own portfolio with lots of effort and to use new technologies and be innovative
Clients	Getting to be creative every day
Client limitations	Being paid to be creative
Trying to explain what you do to extended family	Creative freedom, helping people realise the potential in their ideas, visual translation

Worst	Best
Sometimes I wish I was doing something that made more of a positive difference to the world, physically	I get to do what I love, I've tried not being a designer and I was really unhappy
The intimacy of sharing what you create with the rest of the world	When that rest of the world responds well to it
Worries about getting work	The work is enjoyable and creatively fulfilling
Clients	The challenges of being able to make something visually appealing and understandable to others
People undervaluing what I do because they don't understand it / can't see it with design eyes	Having a job I love
That the subject is often undervalued or misunderstood by clients	That it is possible to make a valuable contribution beyond the world of design
That the work is never done	The variety of subjects / projects that challenge all aspects of one's intellect, creativity and communication skills
	Generating ideas, research, making stuff
Lack of sleep	I can make a difference
Misunderstanding of the skill / effort required in work output, and stressful deadlines	Doing what you love every day! Problem-solving and new challenges
Being insecure about your own capabilities as a designer	In the work I do, I try to combine being a designer with being an editor, and occasionally a writer and photographer – as a book designer you get to put all of these elements together
Instability	Creativity and variety

Worst	Best
Everyone you know, from any career or background, wanting work from you for free	Opportunities to be creative and commercial at the same time. Also, everyone needs to be able to sell themselves in business. We have the tools, skills and creative eye to know exactly how to make ourselves stand out
The pressure to be innovative and artistic	Every project is a different challenge
Low pay	Creative satisfaction
The majority of work being digital	Being creative
Having to keep quiet when people who aren't designers talk about 'design'	I get to make things look good all day
The internal struggles	When you get a great idea
Not getting paid enough. Or people expect you to work for free because you are doing something 'creative'	The times when it feels like play, when you think, 'I can't believe someone is paying me to do this'
Clients assuming they know how to do your job... as if because they have colour preferences, all your training is useless	Making beautiful things
Seeing the details in everything	Seeing the details in everything
Having to sit down all the time	Making things that make sense
The majority of your time being spent behind a desk	Getting to learn about different subjects / industries, etc in order to design something for them
Working in visual customer service	Seeing the world through a designer's analytical eyes
Facing the attitude that anyone with a copy of Photoshop is a graphic designer	Being able to make a living creatively

Worst	Best
The obsessive behaviour of checking, checking and checking again	Achieving good work that is sensitive to both the content and the audience
Long hours when there's no reward, ie an idea gets rejected	Learning. Finding out something new about a subject and doing something creative with it
Lack of clear briefings within the business... and being frustrated with yourself for not being able to find the right answer quickly enough	Being paid to be creative
Never switching off	Creating things
The fact that people expect it to be your whole life if you want to be successful	The creativity
People assuming you do it because you're not academic / can't do anything else	Always learning
It is easy to question the worth of your work to society	Some days, when the project you are passionate about is going right, nothing could feel better
Pandering to clients	Problem-solving
It's hard to get into	
Not being listened to	Nurturing emerging talent
Not being able to mentally detach from your personal design projects	Not being able to mentally detach from your personal design projects
Some clients	When clients are pleased with my work. Earning money while being creative
Negotiating fees	Finding solutions
Sitting at a computer	Every day, I think how lucky I am to be doing this – it is a privilege

Worst	Best
Long hours, unpredictable	Creative
The rest of the world rarely understands or appreciates what we do	Helping the rest of the world understand and appreciate what we do
None	Communication and working with language, learning new information through researching
Back pain	Fun work
Not being able to watch or look at / appreciate any kind of design work without analysing it	Creative freedom
Everyone thinking they are one	Getting to work with colours and create real things
Nothing	Learning new things
People [non-designers] think they can do your job, which is hurtful as it dismisses your talent	The satisfaction you get from completing work that you worked hard on and is admired by yourself, your colleagues, the client and others
Clients not agreeing with you	Having the freedom to be creative every day
Clients	Typefaces
Clients thinking they know better than you	Producing something that exceeds the brief and engages people
Contentless contrivance within the industry and underrated misconceptions from outside the industry	Exploring any and all curiosities – being a designer doesn't / shouldn't ever limit you to one interest or subject matter
Being 'art directed' by clients	The variety of subjects you can deal with and the boundaries you can cross
How subjective the field is	Creating something people will enjoy

Worst	Best
Lack of credibility	Freedom, to a certain extent
Not many appreciate or respect what it is that we do, and so don't see much value in it, especially when it comes to time and money	I can change and evolve all the time, and get away with being 'weird' and 'quirky'
The pressure of being creative and competitive	That you can work and be in touch with lots of interesting people from various fields
Lack of understanding by clients of what we do and the value of it, and the constant need to communicate that	Receiving that design you're proud of back from the printers and seeing that it worked well
My current job. Or unemployment [I can't decide which is worse]	When you get in 'the zone', designing something you're proud of. The chance to make broad cultural associations and have a myriad of sources inspire and inform your work
How commercial the projects have to be so that you can make a living	Being creative
Never feeling good enough – even if it's the best thing I've ever done, it's still not good enough, there's always more, always. That, combined with being on the constant search for criticism like some kind of masochist, means many sleepless nights	Despite this, I wouldn't change it for the world. It's the job I dreamed about as a child, I just didn't know the name for it. You know when you're having a bad day and designing something and it just doesn't work, you've tried everything... but it's just not right. It's over half way... you force yourself to have a break, come back and give it another go, and suddenly... it works... you moved one tiny thing and the whole thing works! It works! That feeling is unparalleled
Clients and the public blame you when things go wrong, and everyone has an opinion	Creative satisfaction; the knowledge that what you make will be used / seen by thousands of people and that your design will hopefully help them
Family always wanting to use your services	Learning about many different industries through a diversity of clients

Worst	Best
If you can't find the right clients to work with, or working environment to be in, it is hell	You can create a small micro-world within the things you design
Being a type designer means that people who can judge and appreciate the quality of the work are usually other type designers [competitors]. People who can give you the job are generally clueless	Great freedom, even in a fairly constrained job
Admin	The diversity of subject matter to work with
The computer	Creative expression and solving the problem
Clients' destructive feedback	Getting to do what I love every day
It's difficult to increase your income without expanding your company. Some jobs can be a bit dull	It opens doors to every industry. I love the project-based nature of the work and discovering new things with every project
My parents not understanding what it means and thinking it just means 'working with a computer'	Working creatively around like-minded people
Having to convince other people that design exists / matters / is powerful	Having my hands on the controls of visual culture
Nothing is ever truly complete – it can always be improved	The freedom and possibility to create something new and original
People not knowing what graphic design means	Creative thinking
Clients	Seeing your work in use
Shit design, labels	Expanding others' curiosity
People not understanding what you do	Getting to be creative every day

Worst	Best
Having to educate clients all the time	Every day is a challenge / joy
No one gets it perfect, and for me, it is not productive to look at the 'worst things' long enough to let it become a 'thing'	It can be so many things, I can carve the path that I find most interesting
Outdated tastes of bosses	Creatively enjoyable work and the occasional moments of creative freedom
Being occasionally forced to work in Microsoft Word	Seeing beauty in type [and type is EVERYWHERE]
Never being able to switch off. That people just think you draw	The creative freedom, and being part of creating everything that surrounds everybody
The fact that your profession is entirely ideas-based and, until you come up with or develop that idea, you're basically useless. Quite a lot of pressure to come up with something amazing	Once / if you do come up with something amazing, it's incredibly rewarding
Lack of time to think	The making process
The fact that people look down on you	Being able to do what you truly love
Lack of creative freedom in commercial work	Making things that were previously awful look nice
Never switching off	Being creative every day
Unpredictable income	Getting to occasionally design
No limits	Creativity
Inconsistency	Creativity and attention to detail
Stress / pressure	Creativity / doing something that brings happiness

Worst	Best
Working hours	Amazing job
RSI	Daily variety
	Not having to satisfy my own criteria, but someone else's
People ask you questions like, 'what is your favourite Pantone colour?' – ie people see it as about decoration, not about problem-solving, thinking or communicating	That you're not limited in what your work might be about
Gender inequality in the workplace	Expressing yourself through design
Low pay for long hours and never having time to work on your own promo as you're too busy working for clients / full-time job	It's the dream
Subjectivity	When my work makes people happy
There are too many of us	Being able to create beautiful things for other people
Working with non-designers, I think it is sometimes frustrating having barriers on creativity	I enjoy doing it, I almost find it therapeutic within the place that I work
Clients who don't know what they want	Seeing your work in print
Designing wedding invitations for friends who have very picky boyfriends	Doing something I love and am passionate about every day
Having critics / clients who know nothing about design and have the final say	Coming to work and getting paid to let your ideas run wild, and discussing them with like-minded people
Finally leaving education in the hope of finding that golden opportunity – for some it can take weeks, for others it can take months or years	If you are brave, experimental and put in the hard work – it will get noticed

Worst	Best
The constant need for perfection – never being satisfied with anything	Being able to make the world better, visually
I graduate in a couple of months so, at the moment, I'm worrying about how to sustain my design practice beyond art school	Satisfaction of making artwork that's meaningful / fun / aesthetically pleasing but also functional as a communication tool – being expressive but solving a problem at the same time
A lot of work, so little time to complete it. Or getting a brief you don't like but you have to force yourself to overcome it and just do it	The freedom that we actually have in terms of the digital world and print. The people we get to meet
Long hours	Long hours
Solitude / lack of sounding board	Relative autonomy – much less stressful working life
It's difficult to know how long things take as every job is different, so constantly doing overtime and people changing briefs. Some tend to think that it's not really a professional job and some aren't prepared to pay but expect a lot	Meeting so many interesting people and always learning about new businesses! Having creative freedom and being able to make
There is no right or wrong answer	It comes from within you. It's part of you
Never being satisfied with finished products	Being creative
Clients / non-arty people not understanding the amount of work that goes into everything	The feeling when you finish an amazing piece
The pay sucks, and sometimes I think people outside the industry can undermine the job role of a designer	It's creative and mentally stimulating in equal doses! And the work can be extremely varied in content
Sometimes people don't understand the creative direction	I get to create and design for a living

Worst	Best
Clients who don't know how to brief	Creating beautiful and useful things
Caring too much	Caring so much
Too much competition	Designing
Non-designers thinking they could do your job easily	Giving life to an idea
Deadlines	Creating new things
Being underestimated	Communicating values
Doing things for no reason	Thinking of creative solutions to help solve problems that benefit the audience
	A unique way of looking at everything – from the way milk bottles are made to the layers and colours of an onion
Having to pare back your ideas for reasons that don't seem to make sense or be relevant	Creative thinking and working with like-minded people
AMENDS	Creative freedom when you get it
The arguments, and it's too competitive	Recognition and respect
Low pay, commercial compromise, clients	Colleagues, studio atmosphere
Being overly self-critical	Creativity and passion
No one takes you seriously	I get to wear trainers to work
People not taking you seriously when you tell them that's what you do	Being able to be creative on a day-to-day basis. As a freelance designer, having the flexibility – financially and time-wise – to travel pretty much whenever I want or have breaks that allow me to travel

Worst	Best
The stress. Being an intern, I get strung along by companies with false promises that there may be a job at the end. Everyone then ends up saying, 'we would hire you if we had a position – you're great'. But there aren't any positions. I'm considering freelancing as I'm currently being given the same responsibilities as a junior, just being paid a peasant salary	Working on real projects and seeing them go live. Even though your name isn't on it and no one else knows, I can go and see the real thing out there and say, 'I did that'
	Fulfilling life ambitions
Having to also be an editor. And having people think they could do your job	Solving problems
The hours you work	The people you meet and work with
The hours	Creative freedom
Constant wearing down from clients who ask for 1,000 variations	Seeing your work complete and executed wonderfully
The desk	Solving problems
Not switching off	Looking for patterns
Back and neck tension from too much screen work	Seeing a project come to life and making the viewer [including the client] happy
Making something beautiful and having a client ruin it	Being able to like my job. Making a living out of what I studied
Hardly ever having opportunities for full creative freedom, and designing logos	The pay can be good, and being surrounding by creatives
Having the feeling of being an impostor very often, and that the fraud police is going to get you because your job is not a proper job	Doing interesting work that's always renewing itself, having the possibility to grow and get better throughout your entire career, being able to work in a lot of different areas, meeting fascinating people

Worst	Best
Non-designers believe that design is as easy as clicking a button and believe that it is ok to ask designers to work for free or barely any money	Being creative almost daily
Working late has now become cool	Variety
‘Do you know where I can buy some cheap templates to make my own posters?’	The dialogue with a commissioner who’s on the same page as you
Clients who ask you to do nonsensical things. It’s harder to take an amend that doesn’t make sense than one that restricts the creative aspects of a piece of work	Learning about different businesses and organisations, helping them to communicate great work / products / ideas
After-hours deadlines, clients making small text amends late into the night. Even though I say I won’t do this / will charge extra, etc, I always capitulate	It’s potentially an exploration of everything, all manner of things are related, it can be as intelligent as you want it to be. It involves topping up with gallery visits, working with different clients on a frequent basis keeps things fresh, being self-employed in my own studio means I don’t have to work if it’s quiet... so many things
Client sentence: ‘it’s alright, just make it a bit more sexy’	Getting paid for being creative, for taking pleasure seriously
Amends to my work, just for the sake of it, so a client feels they have had an input – infuriating	Earning a living making images
Never knowing when to switch off – everything is design to you	Being able to visually contribute to the world
Taking work home	The opportunities
Workload	Being able to do something you love and earn a living from it
Not producing as quickly as our ideas come along	Having fun

Worst	Best
Questioning everything all the time can be draining	Broadness
Non-designers thinking they can design	Often it doesn't feel like work
I find that a lot of other people within the industry are irritatingly pretentious	The feeling you get after completing an excellent piece of work
Sometimes designers are too self-indulgent and bitchy	Changing perceptions
Insecurity	Freedom to run your own business and getting paid for making things, even if the client interferes
Always being told to make it bigger. Once, in retaliation, I made the logo the entire width of the monitor and sent that back to the client. They found it funny, but thankfully asked for it to be made smaller	Being able to work as part of a team to push a project through to completion. It feels incredibly rewarding to take something through from conception and be able to deliver the final solution to the client
Not being able to pinpoint one particular skill set	Not being able to pinpoint one particular skill set
The rapidly and ever-changing design scene. People thinking that because they can learn a software programme, they are also creatively capable and can give guidance to clients, which is not the case	It's part of your life, you never leave it at work. Design is everywhere
Bad kerning ruining a perfectly good day	Currently – all of the possibilities
Thinking about design all the time	Thinking about design all the time
Creative block	Finished projects and great clients
Starting with nothing, building something	It's time-consuming

Worst	Best
Non-designers. People who think it holds little value	When you impress yourself with what you have created
Always having to learn	Always having to learn
Research	Finished outcomes
People often ask for things for free. You'd not ask a builder to build you a house for free	To be able to create something that benefits someone else in some way
Money	Nothing
Not getting your own way	Making things beautiful and functional
Picky clients	Bringing an idea to life
Seeing everything	Seeing beauty in every detail
Having to keep up with digital technology changes is to the detriment of design work	Informality, freedom and continuous discovery
Too much sitting down	Creativity
Clients who've no idea about what graphic design is and how it functions	Clients who are clued-up about what graphic design is and how it functions
Nothing	You get to know the latest trends in almost everything… and get to use them in your work. You get to be socially active
Ignorant clients and tedious production processes	The rewarding feeling when you produce work you are truly satisfied with
This endless survey	
The pay	The glorious outcome, particularly when you know you've done your best and it shows

Worst	Best
The bloody hours	Every day you can turn a new page
The unstoppable urge to help people and fix problems	The unstoppable urge to help people and fix problems
	People enjoying what I produce
Still being considered a 'hobbyists' profession' despite the £billions contributed to GDP	It's bloody fun
Everyone else thinks they can do it	Freedom to experiment
That your work is challenged on a subjective level by people who don't understand the brief	You can illustrate ideas in a way that non-creative people can easily understand
Money talk with clients	Creative output as work
Competitive market	Nailing a brief, where both the client and I are really happy with the end result
Working to an unclear brief	Successfully solving a tricky design challenge
Dealing with rude people who don't offer 'constructive' criticism	Working with a diverse range of people on a broad range of projects
Lots of admin, and the negative impact of marketing departments on graphic design work	Seeing your work in the world, and working with great people on collaborative projects
Everyone thinks they are one	Problem-solving
Short deadlines	Creativity and freedom
Most people don't know what it means	Generally enjoying my work
Varying expectations of what a designer actually does	A fulfilling creative brief

Worst	Best
Most of the creative people I've met / managed / worked with in London are uncreative twats with zero ambition and because they can use a computer they think they are better than carpenters	I am creative enough to lie
Long hours	Colouring in
It's something that is also a good thing... the mix of pure creativity and commerciality	Creating
It's insignificant	Making cool shit
The expectation and perception of our profession	Cool as fuq
Being expected to respect a very junior and inexperienced member of client-side staff, who talks crap that you have to enthuse about	Producing work that totally reinvents a brand for the better
Busted eyesight	
Marketing teams who do not understand their job	Realising the big idea, and delivering it
When the client puts quality and principles last	All of it
A lot of time sat in the same space, too much screen time	You can use your imagination to create beautiful and functional items that improve the world around you
Not being able to not judge pretty much anything based on its purpose, design and execution	Being able to judge pretty much anything based on its purpose, design and execution
People	In the North ... plenty of work
Being asked your favourite Pantone colour	Constantly changing work. Free creative rein. Creative daily activities that rarely get stagnant

Worst	Best
Deadlines, and people who think designers will do everything for free because it costs nothing to make a logo, etc	Creating a successful brand and website
Last-minute changes	Mind freedom
People don't understand what I do	Seeing your work out there, doing well for your client
Being overworked. And everyone thinks they're an art director	It's fun and something I keep learning to get better at
Suppliers	Doing what I love as a career
Not being paid	The design is more of a hobby than a job, and being my own boss
Constant criticisms	Freedom. Showing your true self
Feedback / tweaks / compromising	Making shit look good
The competition, being stuck at a desk all the time	doing what you enjoy for a career
Not being able to read magazines – and only being able to scrutinise the editorial design	Becoming a mini expert in a topic for every new project. It means you know a lot about some obscure subjects
The amount of ideas never used	Always different, always a challenge creatively
Not being understood	Not being understood
Most people don't see it as a highly skilled profession	If you like art and you are lucky you can have lot of fun doing what you love
Explaining to people why we charge for it and don't do it for free	The buzz that comes from doing something that you are happy doing, and seeing your ideas being used to engage with people

Worst	Best
As a student, worrying because the career is so competitive	The creativity, making something better than anyone else could
Not being able to switch off, and being hyper-critical	Being creative is the most enjoyable outlet
Some clients	... the other clients
Abundant competition	Following a passion for creativity is a legit career option
The solitude it can bring	The beauty that can be created
Potentially little income as a job	It doesn't feel like work
Questions like the one above	Solving interesting problems – varied work every single day
Reaching a creative block and struggling to do good work	The sense of achievement and clear finished product at the end of a project
Lack of integrity in companies	Creating
Professional snobbery	The office environment
Career opportunities	Creative problem-solving
Dangerously curious mentality, which may well have me killed one day. The inability to believe anything in the modern world – 'definitely Photoshopped...'	Being able to have such an enjoyable and satisfying work life and daily routine
Not being able to fully realise your idea	Actually being happy about your work for once
Underpaid	Colouring in for a living
How pretentious the industry is, only hairdressers have more awards ceremonies	Influencing people's decisions on a daily basis

Worst	Best
Never quite being good enough or entirely satisfied with your work	Continuously learning and progressing as a designer and a developer is both fascinating and exhilarating
Lately, other designers lending their opinions on social media	I get to smell paper a lot
Proliferation of egos	Making stuff
CREATIVE LIMITATIONS BY THE CLIENT. SITTING DOWN ALL DAY	WE GET TO CREATE THINGS FROM SCRATCH
The above question	I'm pursuing something I set out to pursue when I was 17 and maintaining it [just about]. I'm able to engage with the life of my time, and I get paid actual money to move things around a screen until I'm happy with how they look – it's confusing, it's frustrating, the culture is full of dickheads and individuals rarely explain themselves, but deep down I still think it might be one of the best jobs in the world <3
Self-doubt or creative block	When you get that 'eureka' feeling
Time and financial constraints placed upon you by the sales person. Boring briefs	Other designers / developers
Having to tell people you're a graphic designer	It's not really a job
Clients thinking I care about their project as much as they do	Not taking things too seriously
The initial push to get yourself out there	The wide range of areas that can be participated in
To justify your choices to design-illiterate people	Every day is a very different day
Not being understood and being undervalued	Seeing your work in use

Worst	Best
Designer culture – postmodern irony, pseudo intellectuals taking things too seriously, North / South [London] divide, 'iconic' designers who spend more time talking about themselves than designing	Private work in my own space
Not being taken seriously	The freedom, the creativity, the youthfulness
Being stereotyped	No one dies if you make a bad decision about a font. Well, actually, I guess they could
Having to use a computer for most of your working day	Solving everyday problems in interesting ways
Never switching off	Never switching off
Dealing with clients who don't understand the design process or appreciate its value	Freedom and creative problem-solving in general
Stress	Beauty
Not being able to switch off from the subject	Playing with typography
Everyone else thinking they are a designer, then suddenly being asked a question, followed by, 'you're the expert'	Not having to use spreadsheets or understand budgets
Too much competition	It never gets boring as you are always working on different projects every day
Self-doubt	Creativity
Comic Sans jokes	Nailing a brief
Over-thinking	Over-thinking

Worst	Best
Chasing invoices	Getting excited
Spending a lot of time alone	Working alone. Being able to read and listen to podcasts and music while I work. Being able to turn down work and pick my own hours
The public perception that we sit around artworking flyers and business cards. Design is about problem-solving	Meeting new and interesting people, and being able to do something I love for a living
Compromise	The people and the working environment
Everyone is the same, dresses the same, eats at the same places, listens to the same music	You get paid to pick colours
Grinding out everyday work [corporate PDFs, medical leaflets, staid infographics] while the design world celebrates nothing but the privileged few who work at Saatchi & Saatchi and the like. If graphic design were a person it would be a vain, Z-list celebrity, fixated on making a name for themselves while their underpaid lackeys run around doing their laundry	No two days are ever the same
Working alongside idiot marketing staff who think they are designers and attempt to sabotage every aspect of the artwork for egotistical and personal reasons	Seeing your work being a part of the world around you
Not being able to switch off; design is all around us	Being creatively rewarding
Self-doubt	Self-directed projects
Clients, who assume about most jobs 'this will only take you five minutes'	The moment of finding the 'perfect' solution, whether it has taken five minutes or 500

Worst	Best
Filling in surveys	Being creative
Bad client interactions	Satisfaction of seeing completed, live projects
Making creative sacrifices for the sake of time / budget / client opinions	When it all goes well, it means client satisfaction and personal job satisfaction
Pay	Computery times
Not enough exposure to sunshine	You get to make things from nothing
Bad clients	Creating
Being undervalued	Creative profession
CLIENTS	CREATIVE FULFILMENT
Everyone is now a graphic designer	I'm interested in it
Fighting for your design	The rare moments when your design goes ahead unchanged
Working with marketing idiots	Working in an informal atmosphere – ie music in the studio, casual clothes
Stupid clients	Getting a good job back from press
Having to explain your work	Variation of work
Making stuff that doesn't look too good	Making stuff that looks good
Long hours	Creative fulfilment
Pay	Creating
Company politics	Making a living creating

Worst	Best
A designer's time, budget and personal pay cheque are all undervalued by clients	The culture of hard-workers and socially savvy people means the majority of designers are interesting to get to know
When they don't buy the idea	When they buy the idea
People think it's a service you will happily provide for free. Most people do not understand what it is, usually thats it's 'websites and stuff'. Everyone thinks they can design a logo	It's nice to put the detail in, to recognise when something has been designed by a designer or not. The work-life balance [for me] and being my own boss and keeping my own hours
Difficult to achieve financial freedom	Solving design problems by expressing your creativity on a daily basis
The fear that you may be redundant	The ability to communicate through visual language
Constant self-questioning	Sense of creative fulfilment
Long hours / stress	Solving problems
The fact that there is no right or wrong with what we do. Everything we create is subject to a higher opinion and, more often than not, that higher opinion will be paying for your work	Expression, and this is one of the few careers where you can truly do something that you 'love'
The gap: vimeo.com/85040589	Solving problems, coming up with useful ideas
Not having enough time	Producing something you're proud of
Explaining what you do to others in small talk	Working with other people
Unnecessary changes. Design by committee	The blank page. Reading into a subject / sector
Most people do not get it	That you see the world differently to the public

Worst	Best
Explaining to people what it is you actually do	The variety of work
Having your work being seen as simple, easy	Being able to work at something I love while listening to great music and generally being left alone
Indecision	The end result
Clients	Clients
Wordpress, etc... client and workplace superiors', preconceptions about how easily or quickly work can be turned around	Getting to do something you enjoy, feel passionate about and that brings you fulfilment through the communication of an idea
The panic at an empty page, the pressure of an empty page and no ideas to show	Being able to create, to make, to bring something beautiful into the world but for someone else, that's very satisfying
Many hours working for something that is sometimes so meaningless	It's a creative job
Knowing that things could always be better	Doing what you enjoy
The vagaries of taste	Making change happen
Emotional roller coaster	Feeling great going to work
You never switch off	You never switch off
Filling out surveys	Procrastinating
Annoying clients who want everything bigger	Being able to visually see your creativity
Hours	Work
As a self-employed designer, the unpredictable earnings. And the lack of freedom sometimes to do what you want	Being creative, having cool things and using a Mac all day. Not having to wear a suit and be bored in meetings

Worst	Best
The misunderstanding of how long things take and how much thinking / knowledge / talent is required. Thus, we're underpaid as an industry	The opportunity to be creative, fresh briefs and challenges that make your job constantly interesting
Finding the balance between speed and quality	The satisfaction of creation
Clients with no clue about design trying to tell a designer to make a change, with no valid reason other than that they prefer it	Using design to develop the world in a way that makes change for the better and helps speed up the time it takes them to consume content
Customers	Customers
Bad clients treating us as production monkeys for their ideas	The challenge of a new brief
Clients	Problem-solving
Clients expecting you to build Rome in a day for pence	Creative challenges and making beautiful work
Explaining your design decision to non-designers	Being able to be freely creative and work on cool projects
Producing commercial rubbish	Being allowed time to reflect on a project / problem
The hours: not being able to leave my work in work, ie thinking about it after hours	The variety
Stress; having to work to extremely short deadlines	Generally doing something that I enjoy for a living
Working with visual illiterates	In the land of the blind, the one-eyed man is king
The hours and the competitive nature of the profession	It's everything, it informs all areas of your life, and I love that
Long hours / poor wages	Enjoying my work

Worst	Best
Long hours – always having to adapt to keep up	The challenge faced with every client
Repetitive, dull work for clients who think they could do better anyway	Discussing a brief and getting carried away with the possibilities of new ideas
Always sitting in front of a computer	The culture, the creative buzz when it happens and an enhanced awareness of visual things
Not being able to switch off	Enjoying your work and having something to show for your efforts
The salary and lack of bonuses, etc	Seeing the final result
The amount of disciplines one job may involve can result in being underpaid	Multidisciplinary
Knowing better	Knowing better
Analysing every piece of design I see instead of enjoying it	Being able to create beautiful things
Constant change	Constant change
That others assume you only care about the way things look	The subject areas, people and places it can put you in touch with seem limitless
Everyone *thinking* they're a designer	Creating something you're proud of
Having to go against what you know works best to get work signed off	Fairly easy-going unless you have a bastard of a client and even then, the challenge of overcoming that can be fun
Ideas being diluted and torn apart before release	Creative freedom and endless possibilities
Uninformed negativity from outside parties	Creation

Worst	Best
Joint first – clients dismissing the importance of design; agencies' / designers' wholesale copying of other designers' work	Being creative, then watching your work come alive in print and / or online
Having to explain what you actually do	Creating
Analysing everything that has been designed	Being able to analyse everything that has been designed
Dealing with clients	The diversity of the work; being able to apply the trade to many different subjects
Over-analysing life	Ability to learn from a million different sources
Never being satisfied with any work produced	Being creative daily
Sitting down all day	Creativity
Pressure	Designing
Graphic design is associated with leaflets and brochures	Helping explain things
	A chance to explore ideas
Nothing is negative	Everything
There are plenty of things. The worst thing is clients who lack trust or refuse to work collaboratively	Seeing a series of thoughts, ideas, discussions and decisions come together to form something coherent and [hopefully] beautiful is very, very satisfying
Not many people understand that design needs knowledge to be practised	
Too much time in front of the computer	Making a living from design

Worst	Best
It is an immature discipline, it lacks intellectual rigour and critical capacity. Consequently, it lacks status as a discipline and doesn't pay well	It has the potential to connect, transform and illuminate the social, cultural and political base
When everything fuses together and you create something rubbish	When everything fuses together and you create something great
Being able to see that most things are horribly designed and not having any ability change that	Making beautiful things and getting people to use them instead of horrible things
Not being allowed to create, or being asked to do jobs that have nothing to do with design	To create something unique that solves a problem or creates a great brand to function in the commercial world
Having to notice bad work around you	Being able to fix things
Having to work with clients who want you to 'make it red', or 'make it pop'	I get to be around nice people all the time and create beautiful things
Seeking clients / work	Doing the job I love and getting immersed in creativity in everyday life
Constant creativity	Constant creativity
Ego	Being paid to be creative
Expectations of time schedules / deadlines	The potential to create something useful
Fairly low pay	I love the work I get to do
To be good at design, you have to think that design is very very important, but it isn't	Making something from nothing
Not getting paid for the hours you actually work	Not being appreciated
Not being able to switch off completely, ever	Most days I can learn something new or sharpen my teeth for the next challenge

Worst	Best
The difficulty of finding a career	Colleagues
How little we are valued as an industry	I get to make beautiful things
Being undervalued by clients, the 'everybody can do your job' attitude [when they clearly cannot!], 'can't you do this for free / next to nothing?'	Finding different and creative solutions for a broad range of problems
The inconsistency of how studios are run, no matter the distance or size	I have no B-plan
Nothing	My view of the world as a designer
Difficult clients	Helping people to communicate
Writing very broadly, the industry [in Britain at least] is maybe a bit obsessed with heroes and personalities, and not interested enough in its own progress or role in society	The satisfaction of making something physical and watching people use it
Clients	Clients
Fading eyesight	Other graphic designers
My boss	Studio Nerf wars
People not realising how much work, time and skill goes into creating something	We create
Insecurity about the future	The ability to work on your own. Freedom
Long hours	You get to learn about a lot of other professions, subjects and people
Developers and media planners, and Microsoft Word and PowerPoint	Getting paid well to do something I would do for free
So far, explaining what I do to the family	Showing what I do

Worst	Best
It's so complex	It's so complex
Not being able to be as creative in projects for clients as I can be in my own personal work	Every day, I get to play
The barriers to accessing non-freelance employment – the UK industry is too London-centric and expects graduates to do unpaid placements before they stand a chance of a junior-level job	Seeing a finished project in context with a happy client; knowing that your input has helped to improve the way their message is communicated
Coming up with new ideas	People appreciating your work
Everybody outside design thinks you are a commercial whore and nothing compared with an artist	Doing a job that is creative and that gives satisfaction
I often feel guilt	It is enjoyable
The clients	The fun
Sitting down	I love type and Illustrator
NO OFF SWITCH	NO OFF SWITCH
Having to explain what a graphic designer does to people outside the creative industry	I'm part of a career path with so many avenues to explore and I'm assured by the fact that a machine could never do what we do
The egos	Producing work that I enjoy
Health	Freedom
Questions like, 'what's your favourite Pantone colour?'	Doing something you actually enjoy and having the ability to make change
Higher likelihood of panic / anxiety / esteem issues	Building
Losing sleep over microscopic points of detail; being the victim of inconvenient inspiration	Realising that there are a lot of ways of being a designer

Worst	Best
The gap between personal interest and the scope of commercial projects	Bringing an idea to life
Self-criticism	Being able to earn a living at something I love doing
Being freelance, you do need to 'suffer for your art' a bit and sacrifice a lot of personal life stuff	As a book cover designer, it's mainly that you have something physical to show for all your efforts at the end of it, and that it might inspire someone in the same way you were inspired to create it
No unions. Freelance precariousness	Interdisciplinary work
Nagging dissatisfaction with my output	Wrestling with a problem – I liken it to unpicking a lock, and when it finally opens the sense of elation [and relief]
The internal knot of uncontrollable rage when seeing badly kerned type	You can make a good living doing something enjoyable
Everyone thinks they could do your job easily, if only they had the time and a fast computer	I understand how the things I love are made and why I'm right to love them
Explaining what you do. Disrespect from clients and assumptions made about your role	Flexibility, creativity, interesting [sometimes] challenges, being kept on your toes
Being asked what a designer does	It's pretty cool, isn't it
Explaining what you do	Changing people's lives
The obsession with the field	The obsession with the field
It's my entire life	It's my entire life
Lack of empathy for what we do	Improving, creating and observing how that output is digested
Everyone else thinking they can do it	Being able to prove they can't. The achievement of slowly making the world look a little bit better

Worst	Best
The inevitably long working days, and the misunderstanding / devaluation of design	Every project brings new content, you never stop learning
Being asked your favourite Pantone colour	Flexibility and change
You never switch off	You never switch off
The fact there are so many 'trend' designers. I'm bored of bad, hashed designs and designers	Ability / thought process
Hard to switch off	Creative and relaxed personality
People asking what your favourite colour is ;)	Dream / thought expression
Creative block	Being given freedom and visually communicating an idea
Other people not 'getting it'	Being able to create things myself
Dealing with awful clients	Making a positive difference to the world
Time spent on work is not reflected in income received	A lot of people still don't know what it means
Brand guidelines	Freedom
The unquantifiable nature of it all, eg how to put a value on an idea or how you can put hundreds of extra hours into a project for no extra cost	Being able to create things, come up with ideas and see them come to fruition, often in the public sphere
As an intern, an unpredictable future	Designing things that people think are cool
Staring at a screen all day	Materialising your designs into something tactile and tangible
Clients	Creativity

Worst	Best
RSI	Indulging my obsessions
Choosing Pantone colours	Blue
Having to deconstruct concepts and justify every decision	Feeling very privileged
Not having enough time	Making the world a little more attractive with each piece of work
A lot of people thinking they know how to 'design' just because they have the software. The public perception of graphic design	The job. The problem-solving. The feeling you get when you complete a job you are proud of
The rate of pay, how hard you have to work with little return, how much time it takes up [you can't just finish at 5pm if the work isn't complete], plus there is always more work. The competition, and how poorly interns and junior designers are treated in some studios	Good graphic design can communicate a message in a much stronger way than any other industry. So if you have something to say that can have a positive effect on the world it can be heard and have influence because of design
Pretentious questions	Doing something creative every day, no two of which are the same
Late payments	Freedom
Clients you have to deal with rather than work with	Doing what you enjoy
The huge range of quite distinct professional lives encompassed by the term	That you operate in a constantly changing field where contemplating how people think is paramount
Having to please everybody	You get to touch and know about almost every industry there is
The power of design, and its worth to society, [as a cause for good or otherwise] is undervalued and not fully recognised	Designing
Not being regarded as a professional	Creativity

Worst	Best
	Creativity
Clients	Communication
The limitation / preconception of the term 'graphic design' and perceptions / assumptions about its value	Flux and shifting paradigms / collaboration / building relationships / talking to people / audiences / working in rich and diverse contexts / adding cultural value
Constantly changing standards and new learning	Working in something I love and creating things that make people go, 'wow!'
There are too many designers, people have a stereotype that's quite negative because there's just not the quality / consistency	Problem-solving that goes beyond the subject
Big-business bureaucracy	Seeing the finished product
Paperwork	The start of a project
Being lumped in with high-profile celebrity 'designers'	It's a lifelong, continuously surprising, apprenticeship
Perceptions of non-designers	Doing what you love
Lack of understanding of how much thought, research and use of design principles goes into individual decisions at every stage of the process	The variety of work you get to do
Clients' short sightedness	021
The constant feeling that you're not good enough. There are always blogs featuring work that you can only dream about making	The variety of projects and scope for creative ideas
Getting older	Unexpected novel developments

Worst	Best
Being unsure of your ability on a daily basis	Doing different things every day
People who think they know more than I do	Meeting people and learning things
That you're the frontline propagators of capitalism	Doing what the fuck you like
Low pay	Creative life
Working with clients who know better	Creativity
Design infiltrates every facet of my life... I have to endure it, I can't escape it even if I want to	Design infiltrating every facet of my life helps me see the world in an interesting way and meet amazing, like-minded people
Sometimes a lack of appreciation	The freedom of creativity
It's difficult to get jobs and to get noticed	It's fun
Trying to find the middle ground between graphic design and something that 'looks pretty' in the clients' eyes	Being able to manipulate an audience into thinking something by how you present your work
Finding work; compromising good work	Creativity; it's emotionally fulfilling
Lack of appreciation	It's interesting and enjoyable
Having to 'please' others	The beginning of a project, when anything is possible and I feel excited about the work
Listening to other people who think they know how to do the job	Not knowing what the final solution will be until the very end
Sometimes being too low in the chain of decisions	Being naturally interested and intrigued by new things

Worst	Best
Seeing the world as the mess it is – lost opportunities	Seeing the world as the mess it is – possibilities
The long hours	The creativity and solving the problem in the meeting with the client
Difficult to quantify the unseen work behind the end result	The possibilities are infinite
Struggling to get started and the possibility of passion loss	The ability to create work that inspires others
The responsibility of making a difference	Making a difference
All the 'hidden hours' that clients / employers sometimes don't see	Seeing something you've created having a genuine impact for your client – sometimes more so when the client is a small business
	Doing something I love
Can't think of one	It's a good way of looking at the world
Having to be pigeon-holed into 'web', 'graphic' designer, etc – I just design	It's also my hobby
Working with clients who are 'back-seat drivers' – in my area of Oxbridge-dominated publishing clients, this can often seem like a class-related thing fostering a lack of trust – and being treated as a page decorator rather than an organising force behind the text navigation	Being in a position [with knowledge, opportunities or even ego] to make a better version of something
Compromise	When you get to be creative, it's great
Clients who think they are a better designer than you	The chance to create work that people admire
Other designers	Other designers
People think you draw for a living	You get to draw shapes for a living

Worst	Best
Amendments	Learning about subjects that are not directly related to design
The graphic design industry	Working with interesting people to produce something challenging and worthwhile
Non-designers' confusion	Non-designers' confusion
People who think you are just a person who knows how to use a computer very well and uses posher programmes to achieve similar results to them – if they had the same access to the software	Getting paid to do my hobby
Pace of deadlines	Doing something you love
	Producing a body of work
Sitting for hours on end	At its best, being part of a valuable profession that has the ability to influence positive change
Dealing with difficult clients	Creative expression
Being tied to a computer most of the time	Variety
Confidence in your work. Could I have done it better?	Creativity. The process of making things out of nothing. Seeing rather than looking. Problem-solving. Ownership
Low salaries and long hours	Creativity, the people, the atmosphere
Seeing good work go unused sometimes	Researching, ideation, creating things
Having to sit at a desk for most of the day	The constant learning about new things
Your passion / career often being trivialised by the rest of the world	Not conforming to corporate culture

Worst	Best
Losing things that you love in a project because the client doesn't feel the same way as you do	Learning every day and getting better. The constant challenge of trying to do the best you can
Enduring people who aren't	Being someone who is
Friends and family not really understanding what I do	Solving problems
Being a designer	Being a designer
The clichés, such as the last question	Doing a job I really enjoy and have passion for
Having disinterested clients who have no real input other than saying, 'it doesn't feel right, I can't tell you why though'	Freedom to create as an author and to work alongside people who want to make a tangible difference, not just for money
Not being able to not be a designer	Not being able to not be a designer
Clients	Using your brain
Never being satisfied	
Being asked what my favourite Pantone colour is	Thinking
The money	The variety of customers and work
The lack of work outside of London	Creating things that will be around longer than I am
Ignorance about design	Design is brilliant
Constantly thinking about design	Constantly thinking about design
The profession being undermined by people assuming they could do it and they are somehow doing you a favour by commissioning you to do the work	When you have a good client who wants to push the boundaries of convention and understands your process; ultimately ending up with a great product and seeing that product [whatever it may be] realised

Worst	Best
The obsession with critiquing what's already out there	The obsession with critiquing what's already out there
Having to compromise design for clients	The people you work with
It's still a job, and like any job it can be repetitive	Occasional creative freedom; some projects are genuinely rewarding
The hours	You get paid to do your hobby
Sometimes long, unsocial hours	It's a fascinating subject to study, and at times it feels like you're being paid to play and do what you love
People don't understand what you do	
Money	Freedom
Creativity	Creativity
Rejection of ideals and having to make compromises to fit timelines and budgets	Working with awesome clients and making a difference
The workload. Being at the end of the line. Work isn't over until the project is over	Being creative for a living
The industry is totally flawed. Mostly, it is seen as ok to work for free. Although nowadays a lot of people dispute this and say that is wrong, it is still widely accepted that people do free work and pitching and have to undertake unpaid or very low paid internships in order to get anywhere in their career. You wouldn't get a plumber do some work on a property for zero fee because it would look good for him [unless potentially for a mate]. Graphic design can often be seen, even from the perspective of other creative disciplines, as this throwaway skill that can be done by anybody, so why pay one person for it when you can just turn to the next one and get the work for free?	I enjoy it and am truly passionate about it

Worst	Best
Seeing so much bad design in day-to-day life	Making the world a better-looking place
The fact that everyone else thinks they can do what you do because they have Photoshop on their computer / Mac	Getting to see projects you have designed and worked on printed and in shops, etc
Compromise	Getting paid for what you love
Hours	Creativity
Public perception	Possibility
Clients	Clients
n/a	The long hours
Being too committed to the artificial world prevents one connecting with nature, for the observation and understanding of its underlying principles help us into being truly better people	Working across disciplines
Having to make the client happy	Making the client happy
Money	Lifestyle
The hours, and clients not understanding about the hours needed for good design	Making stuff
Nothing	Everything
Blank page	Blank page
Self-doubt in ideas	Creating things
n/a	My hobby as a job

Worst	Best
Angst and dissatisfaction over the inconsequential	Making something that works
Micro-managing creative directors	Doing what you love for a job
People expecting you to work for free because 'it's just a logo'	It's my lifeblood, being creative can be a lot of fun
Having creativity killed because of employment	Mostly everything
Other designers	Other designers
Self-doubt	Being paid to think creatively and solve problems
Nothing	You can make work and express yourself
Being asked what your favourite Pantone colour is	Knowing that it's Cool Grey 10 anyway
Sitting at a computer all day	Sitting at a computer all day
The clients; often the work; always the extended working hours	The rare projects where you have a day and come out with something you're proud of
Computers and desks	Changing things
I don't get to do much work that aligns with my interests, ideas and goals. Monitoring creativity kills creativity	Doing meaningful work that matters and you can take pride in. Helping people build their businesses, and projects that you believe in too. Also, it's a very open profession that can be applied to anything, which is quite rare and cool. The only drag is when it gets applied to things that don't interest you or motivate you, which is a lot of the time in the real world

Worst	Best
Clients / co-workers not understanding that a designer is hired as a designer because they know about design. Saying, 'move this here' isn't feedback, it's pretending to be a designer. I wouldn't tell a strategist how to do their job, so they shouldn't be telling me	There is a possibility to create something I am genuinely happy with. Still chasing that dream
Sitting, looking at a screen for 90% of the day	The feeling when a project goes live
Being rushed	When a client goes with your 'left-field' solution
Whingeing about being a designer	Whingeing about being a designer
Instability and insecurities	Beats getting 'a real job'
Computers	When you finish something you are happy with and no one else has fucked up
Hearing clients telling you that you don't know what you are doing and it should surely be Comic Sans for headlines	Meeting clients who will listen to you and respect your professional opinion. They wouldn't tell a mechanic how to get their car through the MOT
Difficult clients	Doing a job you enjoy
Having to do production work sometimes	Being paid to solve visual problems
Repetitive work	Own projects
Finding the clients who are willing to pay	I can make anything look pretty – including assignments
Being undervalued	Being creative for a living
It's not as fun any more, the Internet has eroded that, it's all there for the taking now. Once upon a time, the exclusivity of specialised knowledge was a nice feeling	Working with like-minded people

Worst	Best
Amends	Not 'living for the weekend'
POOR PAY	IT'S FUCKING COOL
Hard work, long hours, not enough pay / recognition	Producing good design
The decreasing reputation of design; the crappy and expensive agencies; the offshore cheap competition; generally, the decrease of the budgets	Creating beautiful things and getting positive feedback and influencing the visual environment
Being identified as a 'creative' and having to come up with 'ideas'	Being identified as a 'creative' and having to come up with 'ideas'
Monetary challenges and everyone assuming you lack traditional and business intelligence	You get to be creative every day
The sea of self-involved people / egos in the industry	Cracking a brief, and the client loving it
It takes a long time to get established	The creativity
Clients	Being paid to be creative
Having to compromise your creative vision in order to please a client	Getting to do something I'm passionate about every day
Always only dressing up other people's content – whether you agree with it or not	Getting paid
Staring at a screen for long periods of time	Creative problem-solving
When you have account teams who think they are designers or art directors	Working on some great projects for exciting clients
The feeling that you are sometimes promoting unnecessary consumerism	Variety of work and new challenges

Worst	Best
Dealing with design industry egos	Making a difference to clients
Other designers	Doing the work
Client limitations	Seeing designs in the world
Not getting paid well	Creativity
Computer eye strain	Designing
The strive for perfection	The subject you interact with
Artworking	Freelancing
Clients	Creative freedom
Bitchy, backstabbing blokey wankers	Finding people who share your design interests and have a common goal to do fabulous work
	Creativity
You never stop working	You never stop working
How hard it is to get a placement or job in the North East	Being creative and doing what I love as a job
Pay	Creativity
Boredom	Freedom
People think you can knock up a logo in minutes	Every job is different
Time management	Creativity
The work always becomes personal	The satisfaction from a nice job
Creative blocks	Passion

Worst	Best
People thinking you can mock up a logo in one hour	Having the freedom to be creative and do an enjoyable job
You never switch off	You never switch off
The pace of change	It's playful
Clients	Doing what you love
The hours	The creative process
Desire for the constant approval of peers	Communication with the world
No one knows what you actually do	No one knows what you actually do
Unpredictable hours	Doing something you enjoy
Beards, tattoos, fixed wheel bicycles, coffee	Freedom of sorts
People think I'm in IT	I'm creative and contribute to a better world. No really, I believe that
Working with a copywriter :)	It's non-uniform
Low-paid entry as a junior designer	Seeing your work in print / being produced
Keeping up with trends and industry standards	Freedom to design and create
Personal creative pressure	Doing good work

Worst	Best
US respondents	
Non-constructive feedback	Work is enjoyable
Management not understanding the creative process	The creative potential and opportunity for project direction
Subjectivity	The moments I am lost in thought
Gender inequality and long hours	Drawing
Too much email	Shaping content in real time
Control issues	Versatility
Your design solution is always questioned	Communicating an idea
Being lumped in with other designers	Being able to work with great people and learn all kinds of things, and in any context / arrangement you want, whether solo, as part of a big agency, or on a small in-house team
Having to come into an office every day	Being able to support a family
Having to educate clients about basics	Praise after a job well done
Having to find new clients	Being able to lead a life I love
There are far worse professions one could be working in. I'm always grateful to be able to work as a designer	Working beyond the profession of design in collaboration with clients and acquaintances from other disciplines. Lifelong learning
There isn't really anything all that bad about being a designer	Being a graphic designer allows you to work in, and collaborate with, a seemingly infinite range of other disciplines
The unpredictability of finances	Satisfaction of problem-solving

Worst	Best
Competition with other designers, the lack of smaller studios in the city of Chicago, and advertising in general	Typography, having a creative job, seeing projects form from start to finish and being proud of the end results
Nothing	Being creative every day
Constant hatred of my own work :)	Freedom to create and try different things until you find one that sticks
Other designers	Lack of definition of discipline
The paucity of the discourse	It's a great form of contemporary cultural production
No	No
	Interesting, challenging work in which you can constantly learn and expand. And you can take positive action in the world, making things more understandable, communicating ideas, etc
Being a slave to the computer	Being creative every day and solving problems
Other designers	Using creativity to solve problems
Being second-guessed by those who do not care to have an informed opinion	Making a real difference in the lives of those you are trying to design for
Clients	Satisfied users
Having to sell the value of design to those who have not previously considered it	Creating for a living
Your work being rejected	Trying out new things
Having to put a price on my skills	The creative outlet
	Working in-house

Worst	Best
Not enough work	Freedom to travel, constant change with jobs. Hard work followed by no work
Everyone else thinking they're a designer	Being able to create anything and everything
Not having enough time	In many ways, it's like being able to work in a lot of different fields. There's always more to learn, research and explore. Designers really get to explore the extremes of form and content
Getting emotionally attached to certain projects	Every day is something new
Creating something you love / a great design, and then seeing it changed / tweaked / slowly destroyed by the client. Because ultimately the work is for the client and they are paying for it	Making the world a more beautiful place, even if in small ways
Clients feel they are also designers due to the abundance of 'self-design' tools that have been developed	The ability to make someone's experience with a particular product delightful
Clients who don't understand what you're trying to do	When things work out the way you envision them
Burning down a project because 'the client is right' when you know it depreciates the project's value. It's like watching something slowly die of cancer. Can be heartbreaking	When you get to try a new kind of project. But this happens rarely, and over time the 'best things' kind of start to show their flaws as well. Guess I'm in the jaded stage of my career
All the not-designing that is necessary, along with client / budget limitations	The freedom and creativity
Always critiquing everything outside of work	Freedom
Micro-managing art directors who are out of touch	Seeing your hard work / ideas out in the real world
Being seen as less than artists	Helping people

Worst	Best
By today's standards, it is almost a cliché	The opportunity to beautify the world
Having to be very self-assured / confident. Having to succumb to non-designer decisions on a project. Not being respected as an expert in our field. Everyone thinks he or she is a designer	Being able to express myself artistically but in a commercial environment. Getting paid to do art. It's such an interesting career. You are able to dabble in a lot of different subjects, so you are learning as you are designing
Companies want more skills for less experience and pay. Hard to make the transition from print to digital	Making nice stuff
Seeing your work misused and mispresented	Creating from scratch
The competition	It's fun
Being stuck in an open plan office for endless hours of uncomfortable sitting with no privacy, plus having to work with headphones on to keep the noise down	Always something new to work on and learn about
Other people not valuing your work and thinking that's it's 'fun' to draw all day	When other people get it
People considering designers as artists who make decision on whims and emotions rather than theory and strategy	Creating something from nothing. Solving problems for clients that they had not yet identified. Getting to know people
The disconnect between people's perceptions of the profession of a graphic designer, and the actuality. Design is often perceived as elitist fluff with little substance, or just decoration, even today, and this is so little connected with the hard work and compassion and vocational quality of the work. Design, done right, is not glamorous or bombastic but smart and elegant and substantial	Learning about different disciplines in being a translator. Seeing how things connect. Engaging with society in an ever-changing way
Being unemployed	Freedom and support

Worst	Best
Employers in my area do not value designers and pay poorly	The chances you get to be creative
Full-time jobs are becoming less and less available. Agencies are becoming more and more specialized, and the American work ethic is leaving no time to advance a career once you're in the workforce – which is why companies are always looking for fresh out-of-college young designers who've had time and freedom to create more diverse and experimental work	Talking with other designers about design and other shared cultural interests
People assume you have 'all the time in the world' or you can do whatever you want in the middle of the day	Creative outlet daily, and flexibility in work environment
Non-designers tell you what to do and you have no creative freedom due to being a in-house designer	Being creative. Being free doing a job that is showing your aesthetic view. Learning new things. Being different and being curious about everything
Closed-minded clients with bad taste	In my case, being able to work on my own and have the freedom to do what I want
Not getting the credit due for the time it takes to create solutions for clients and so not being paid appropriately for those solutions	Being able to create and apply a visual solution that people can experience
Fighting the urge to work for free simply because you love the work	Solving a problem successfully
When design becomes a task	My work is enjoyable and interesting
Masculine and sexist culture	Being able to challenge this culture
Semi-constant computer work	Communicating visually in a way that people can't do themselves
Competition for work	Creative work, satisfaction of finished work
Web design	Creativity

Worst	Best
Clients	Type / image / form / color / structure in the service of a beautiful concept
People tend not to listen	People tend to just ignore eccentricities
That the profession isn't treated as equal to any other skilled profession. A click of a button, and a logo is done... 'Why does it cost so much?'	The freedom to work on projects you like, and to create. The look on a client's face when it's better than they could have ever imagined
Creating designs you feel are great, but having the design you feel is not as strong be chosen by the client instead	Creating new experiences through graphic visuals
Constant feelings of inadequacy	Occasional breaks in the constant feelings of inadequacy when a job ships
Compromise	Making the world a prettier, easier-to-use place
The disconnect with the rest of the professional world	The fulfilment of truly creating something out of nothing
Flippant clients who consider us decorators	The fun
Non-designers thinking they can design	Tight-knit community
Lack of jobs in management, not getting a chance	Creative fun
Unlimited rounds of edits	Freelancing
People think I design logos	An ever-expanding toolkit
Nothing other than the occasional bad client	I can be entrepreneurial
Stupid clients	You can work for yourself as well as work for others

Worst	Best
People think I just make pretty pictures	I get to do what I love all day
No license or accreditation = no respect and many hacks competing with each other	You are not an accountant
One who doesn't meet the deadlines	You get to learn a lot about different fields
Always being critical of everything. Sometimes you have to learn how to shut it off and enjoy life as it is	It's a very wide-open field. I can work in a factory-style production office, for a packaging firm or even from a cafe half way around the world from my clients
Having to read the client's mind sometimes	The feeling of accomplishment once you finish a project that you worked very hard on
Dealing with people who don't think design matters	Seeing designs in action, seeing that it really does matter
Picky clients	Creativity
The designer's eye never rests	It's built-in cool
Being the last link in the food chain	Being able to learn from so many other fields of knowledge
Educating others about what it is we do and why it is valuable	Seeing people using and interacting with the work
Last-minute changes	Designing
Feeling replaceable in the sea of other designers	Making
Being bored by the work	Being excited by the work
Client limitations and 'writer's block' before deadlines	Making awesome shit
Insecurity	Getting to create

Worst	Best
Lack of involvement in strategy and over-the-shoulder clients / art directors	Getting paid to make stuff, especially for products and causes that you personally believe in – when you can land them
People think that if they have Photoshop then they are a designer, and also people think that you should want to do free work just for your portfolio	Working in a creative field. Making weird stuff for yourself and then finding out other people also love it
Last-minute requests / demands	It's a small but very wide world
Everyone thinks they are a designer and can do better	Not much these days
Frustration of people who don't understand and ask me to do non-design tasks [social media, coding, tech support, etc] and then get angry with me when I explain that's not in my skill set	Using creativity, working on a variety of different projects, stumbling across something I worked on in a store or magazine
Sitting all day, every day	Having reach
Graphic design is now web design and most people think they can be designers because everything is so accessible, which has been limiting employment opportunities as well as salaries	Being able to problem-solve by coming up with new concepts and being able to execute them yourself, or directing someone else to
Working with stubborn, unreasonable clients	Being able to create for a living
The worst thing is the paperwork – budgeting, bids, etc; the things that take away from project research, relationship building and creation	Finding meaningful solutions to challenges that inspire an audience
People don't understand the designer's role, or, they believe anyone can be a designer	I love creating work to benefit others
The lack of respect for your profession	

Worst	Best
Clients	Clients
Thinking that your work should be adding up to something more than it feels like it is	Sometimes I stop and think, 'I am getting paid to do this'
We are perfectionists	We like perfect things
Fighting for aesthetic control when the particulars of a situation mean it will not be given over easily	Having a positive impact on a situation, seeing the effect of your work
The previous question in this survey ['what is your favorite Pantone color?']. Designers obsessed with design culture and ignoring the interdisciplinary and critical aspects of the profession make the discipline of graphic design look like a joke to lay people. 95% of graphic design is unnecessary or pointless	Contemporary graphic design is slowly branching out and dabbling in other disciplines, and that is exciting to be a part of and witness
Being treated as the least important person in the room	Not being something else
Recognising some of the dopey views entrenched within the design industry after taking this survey	It pays for the food on my table
Nobody truly understands what we do, and how important we are	Being able to communicate graphically
Always having to go after the next job	Freedom to be artistic
The lack of respect	Creation and discovery
Everyone wants to be one	Everyone wants to be one
I'm sometimes over-analytical about situations	I learn a lot about how people use things and interact with each other, which is very interesting
Clients who micro-manage	Doing something creative for a living

Worst	Best
Our work impacts on people's lives	Our work can impact on people's lives – for the better
My brain never stops, but really that is not that bad	Design is all around, and every moment something new can inform what I am working on
Endless / thoughtless commodity marketing of useless / worthless products of dubious quality / relevance	I have a fairly concrete skill and portfolio to fall back on, and I get to collaborate with interesting people in all manner of fields, industries and so on. Additionally, it's constantly changing and in flux, which is healthy and exciting in my opinion
Clients' willingness to interfere in a subject they know little-to-nothing about, which is supposedly why I was hired. In no other industry that I've worked has this been the case; they have all been customer-interaction-heavy	Creating a concept from scratch and seeing it come to life
Budgeting time and money, trying to figure out pricing	Thinking through problems as they arrive and learning / figuring out how to solve them – especially figuring out clever and unique solutions
Narrow perspectives of what the title means	The openness to explore ideas and collaborative work with many people in many professions
The clients	The job
Navel-gazing and envy [by other designers]. Lack of understanding [still] by most non-designers that web designers are not window decorators	Since most of what we make ends up in the trash or incompatible with future technical updates, not a whole lot
Lack of business classes in college [UK], being inept at talking money with clients	People seem to think it's a cool profession [I'm not sure they realize how hard it is]
Being awake at 4am	When your idea comes to fruition
Workload	Ability to be creative in a job I love

Worst	Best
Dealing with clients	Designing
Clients	To be creative
Not getting the same respect as developers [and the same pay]. We're just as important to the process as they are, but we aren't always treated that way	Knowing that something you're making is [hopefully] helping someone somewhere accomplish a task, or making their life a little easier
Other asshole designers. Lofty, pretentious community that gets off on making things for themselves and not the rest of the world. Long hours. Being under-appreciated by who you work for / with. Never being 'off the job'	Helping people solve problems. Engaging with an active community around your career that shares many of the same interests as you. Fun, engaging, creative work. Always having to learn something new. Never accepting the status quo. Always being challenged and climbing that metaphorical mountain
The clients	Creative freedom
There are too many of us	Being creative all day, every day
People asking you to work for free, having difficulty establishing your value	The community surrounding the creative arts
Clients	Essentially knowing a different language
Perceived as being less important than an art director	As a designer, I feel that my senses are heightened and I'm more sensitive to experiences and life in general
Narrow-minded clients	Problem-solving while simultaneously creating something beautiful, it works both sides of the brain
Project stress; clients believing all design is simple and quick	The vast array of clients and projects. My peers
Being paid to think deeply about a subject, and in the same breath having those thoughts dismissed due to client preference	Getting to think about shape and form. And the ability to make things better most of the time

Worst	Best
Dealing with people	Expressing your ideas and making them appealing to others
Creative block. The fear that your profession could be done by anyone with a MacBook and Creative Cloud	When you are working on a design and you are psyched about it
Long hours	Freedom
Clients changing your work or not believing in your ideas	Everything
It's boring [to me] and not satisfying	It's somewhat creative and I can make a living out of it
Sitting in front of a computer all day	Living off what you love to do
Liaising over print production	Seeing your work out in the world
Frustration	Solving problems
The never-ending critiquing of one's work. It's never good enough	Getting to learn about all different kinds of subject matter. I love doing research and coming up with ideas
Questionnaires	Designing
The hours	You get to solve problems every day with art, and collaborate with amazingly talented people
Not all environments are conducive to listening to any ideas. The group is small and exclusive	Creating something that is impactful and expressive
I think this is mostly part of self-employment / running your own studio: taxes, organizing your business but not completely knowing how. Being Dutch and recently moving to the US has been stressful because everything is organized differently here, I have to do taxes in two countries, but no one really seems to know how to help me with this	Graphic design being so all-encompassing in my life

Worst	Best
It's supposed to be a cool job, but the reality is you have the same things to deal with in any office job. Not as creative as I hoped and I'm getting tired of being treated like a junior when I've been in the industry for 10 years	When you have a good day, it's great
Dealing with clients who see designers as only a tool	Designing, solving problems and seeing our work out in the world
Other non-designers thinking that it's not important	Being able to think creatively every day and not have every project be the same as the previous one
Mundane tasks such as changing / updating info on flyers / ads	Starting a project where you're the art director and finishing it, having had your hands on multiple assignments [like photoshoots, layouts, etc]
The cult of the personality. That I feel, to stay competitive, I have to have an online persona	Doing whatever you want
People thinking you aren't doing real work, or that things can just come to you without thought or research or sketching. Please! I need some time and thought before I can really come up with a home run on this piece. If you want a thoughtless, two-second logo, fine. But I can, and will, do better with time to work it out	Visualizing EVERYTHING. Once you learn it, it's yours, and the whole world is a visual world full of experience and insight and inspiration. Every design choice matters. Mine, yours and everyone else's – good, bad or indifferent
Inferiority complex	Being able to pitch creative ideas
Working with ignorant non-designers who think that design takes no time at all. They don't understand or respect the process or the time things take	Making things
Being undervalued for our work	The variety of work every day, getting paid for being in the art field and not being a 'starving artist', and problem-solving
How little time you actually spend designing	Seeing your final product on display and achieving [or exceeding] its intended objective

Worst	Best
Can't stop critting work	Creating and experimenting
Never being done – your work can always be better, there are always new things to learn and new things to play with	Never being done – your work can always be better, there are always new things to learn and new things to play with
People often think it's easy to do and / or don't understand it	The opportunity to solve problems creatively
The uncertainty	Knowing it is always needed in any / all communities
Clients who don't understand design and say things like, 'do your magic' and 'jazz it up'	Being able to take someone's boring brief and turn it into a piece of art
Low budgets	Solving problems
Worrying about the impact your work has on society and the world... if it leaves an impact at all	Being able to call work fun
Deadlines	Creating something new and beautiful
Decoding what the client wants and convincing them what they really need	I get to solve problems, make things work better, make them more beautiful and make things work EVERY DAY
Never feeling your work is 'finished'	Being able to create in every imaginable capacity
Not being appreciated by clients [ie when clients take over the design process]	Creative problem-solving
I buy everything because of how it's designed or how it functions digitally	The people I work with. Creatives are weird individuals. It makes for a fun work environment and I'm learning and changing [becoming even weirder] every day
Always selling yourself out	Getting to do creative work with stability

Worst	Best
Clients	Being creative
It's hard to price your work and find clients who are willing to spend the money, and not just get a templated design online	Technology, software and trends are always changing so it never feels old
Caring	Caring
When clients are too conservative as marketeers	Logo / brand concepting
Everyone thinks they are a designer and you are beholden to your client's opinions, so you often have to sacrifice a good design for client happiness	Two things – having a defined skill and having a tangible body of work to represent yourself with
Sometimes things you do suck and you can't really tell why. It's difficult to articulate what makes something successful, which can make it difficult to succeed [but really rewarding when you do]	Creating something you know will make the world a better or more beautiful place
Occasionally, it feels like I'm not doing anything significant. A crisis one day was when two different rich blacks didn't match on press! People are doing heart surgery, and I'm worrying about inks	Getting to make beautiful things that communicate well on a regular basis, or at least having the opportunity to
Being compared with other designers and not being good enough. Trying to find a job as a designer with no design education	Solving problems creatively
Uncertainty about the trajectory of my career	I make a living doing what I'm good at
Being so obsessive with the details that we lose sight of people and the bigger picture	Being multidisciplinary
No one knows what it means	Finding a solution
All the pro bono work requested of me	Being an expert in an area – looked up to by friends

Worst	Best
The superficiality of a lot of what we do / are expected to do / present ourselves as doing	The ability and opportunity to create things that didn't exist before
Everybody thinks they are a designer too	I get paid to make beautiful things
How the design field thinks of itself as being so grandiose and important. Design is important, but it's important because of the messages we convey, NOT because of egos or design itself	You get to meet all kinds of people and learn about many different ideas and concepts, and then use your powers to amplify other people's voices
Hard time explaining colors / types / design to a non-designer	Always being surrounded by fun and interesting stuff
You're never 'done' with a project like a 'normal' job is. Most professions know when to stop a project, like if you're building a house, you stop when the house is finished according to the floorplan. As a designer, however, there's no set end point for a project, which makes it tricky to end	Designers get to comment on society and sculpt the world around them by crafting art with information
Clients underestimating the amount of work it takes	Being able to successfully communicate visually. And making cool shit
No such thing	Help your clients to grow their business and navigate a world so overwhelmed with information
Dealing with ignorant and rude people	Getting into a creative zone and losing track of time
Other designers	Creating art I love for clients I care about
Clients 'dumbing down' your work. Having a great design and them wanting an option that doesn't look as good	Creating work that is seen in the 'real world' in print or digitally. Getting compliments on work
Clients	Creativity

Worst	Best
People don't understand what I do	The diversity of projects
Burnout	Getting to wear a lot of hats, being constantly challenged
	Always learning new things
Being creatively stifled due to client / money / time	Getting to be creative every day, doing what I love and getting paid for it
That most people in the world don't understand the importance of good design	Helping to make the world a more visually pleasant and interactive place
Unmotivated days	Brainstorming with like-minded people; elevating the project to new, previously unimaginable, heights
Designer's block	Seeing finished projects and being proud / getting recognition
Client ignorance as to what we really do	Seeing your work be used to promote something. It gives you a sense of pride
Everyone having a say or being able to give an opinion on your work [but you need a person well-versed in code to give feedback to a developer]	Making things work and look better – woo
Long hours for low pay, sitting all the time, egocentric culture	Learning random new things [perspectives, fields of knowledge] through clients
Having to have previous experience for an entry-level position. Most junior roles require two to three years' experience in the field	Creative challenges
Having to design other people's visions	Being able to create art and bringing ideas to life every day

Worst	Best
Clients	Solving problems
Constantly explaining what you do, which is difficult because we do so much	The chance to be creative every single day
Having to be a jack of all trades, ie you are required nowadays to be a programmer, developer and an expert in all things interactive as well as print	A creative outlet, and always being able to learn and discover new things
Seeing many of those in the same profession become complacent, lose passion and become designers just for the money	Being part of the design community with like-minded people who want to do good
Constant pressure to adapt	Making the man-made world a more beautiful place
Being creative	Being creative
Always looking to make things, processes, ideas, designs better	Aesthetic consciousness
Not enough time to work on personal projects	Doing what I love to make a difference in the world by designing for good causes
It's impossible to see anything without critiquing it	The problem-solving mindset and ability to communicate an idea
Clients	Design is seen everywhere, and everyone can be impacted by a design
Time management	Being able to manage the way others see information
Never being understood / appreciated	Getting to be creative every day
Using printers prone to technical difficulty	Making the world beautiful
People expecting spec work	Getting to be creative at 'work'

Worst	Best
Iterations	Iterations
The feeling that design is subjective and anyone can do it	Creativity and variation
Feeling incompetent, as though I don't have good ideas [or can't get my work to a great place quickly enough]	As a book designer, receiving copies of my work from publishers to display on my shelf is the best reminder of why I work as hard as I do
Missing that sense of truly helping others	I share unique bonds with many of the people I've worked with, both because of our jobs and personalities [which are probably related]
Hard work	Your creativity for others
The public doesn't respect it as an art. Too many people asking for free work because 'anyone can design... all you do is drag and drop'	Creativity! Creating something out of nothing! Making things beautiful
Instability and uncertainty	Creativity
Doing mediocre work for nightmare clients who pay really well	Doing great work for great clients and seeing it out in the world
Clients	Clients
Not being able to turn off the analytical way of looking at the world and just enjoy something for what it is or what it looks like	Looking at the world in an analytical way, seeing why it is the way that it is, and the ways that it could be made better / prettier / more efficient
The stereotype does not convey the extreme variety there is in the 'design' profession	The intense research leads to a simple understanding of a large range of subjects
Not having decision-making power	Proposing simple solutions to complex problems
	Being good at solving problems
Dealing with difficult clients	Designing for money

Worst	Best
The approvals. I work in a corporate environment, which at times can feel a little creatively constricting	Getting to make things, and seeing how they have impact
Noticing bad type treatments everywhere I go	Being able to legitimately impact the world and the way people interact with it. At least for a few people
People thinking everything is free and easy to do	It's fun
As someone who works as an in-house designer [for the past nine years at various organizations], graphic designers rarely get the recognition they deserve. When an event or campaign is successful, it's always because of the project leader or guest speakers, not because of the design	Exercising my creative skills daily. Communicating visually through conceptual ideas that help people to digest content easily
Clients	Creativity
Competitiveness	It's great if you love art
	Creativity
The long, long hours	Constantly learning about about people, processes, new subjects for new clients. Becoming an expert in something you had no idea about two months earlier to be a strategic partner to clients
The assumption that your only contribution is visual	
Insecurity	I am always learning something new
Everyone's a designer	Getting lost in my work
Sitting at a computer	Fluidity
Misperceptions of the role of design	The opportunity for expression

Worst	Best
A desk	Encourages curiosity, new ideas
The unpredictability	The unpredictability
Other shitty designers	Doing the work
Almost everything	Testing clients' anger thresholds when you fuck with them and are being noncompliant with their wishes
Printing	Everything
Design is saturated with many untalented people	Ideas
People don't understand it	People are excited by what you do
Feeling an outsider sometimes	Having a critical view on things
Being devalued as a decorator, not a problem-solver	Access to interesting people, projects and businesses. Working with other creative people
Insomnia	Insomnia
Poor organisation of materials by client	Differing assignments
Keeping up with web design technology	The home runs
Being pulled in too many directions	Coming up with solutions
Clients	Loving your work
Being misunderstood as to what my job entails. Clients estimating how much time work takes me	Being able to draw pictures for a living
Being asked what your favorite Pantone color is	

Worst	Best
The impossibility of detachment from my work	Being able to point to something at the end of the day and say, 'I made that'
There is so much to learn as a young designer to be able to pull off this profession [not just the technical side], and some of it is difficult to explain. Much of it you just have to be exposed for long enough for it to click – makes it a bitch to start off with	My profession and my hobby are the same thing
The constant self-doubt is probably the worst thing about being a designer. It's personal but it's not, if you know what I mean	Seeing a project succeed because of your design decisions
'I can get someone on the Internet to do it much cheaper'	'That is so fuckin' cool'
Deadlines. Ankle-biters. Unimportant projects	Creating beautiful things and getting paid for it
Advocating the need for the profession, as well as fair pay for the profession	The ability to take even the smallest thought in your head and manifest it into something tangible
It is looked at as an art rather than a science. And everyone is an expert	I get to play on Photoshop all day
Clients	The final product
Being asked what your favorite Pantone color is	The chance to be creative
Hours	Creative expression
Working on crunch time	Having the ability to be creative and explore different solutions to a problem
Non-degree designers and spec work	Creative freedom and restraints

Worst	Best
The large number of worthless shitheads	The calibre of the few kind and interesting folks
Dealing with poor clients and / or poor creative leadership	You get to create stuff
Not being taken seriously	Getting to make some of the coolest things people have seen
I work in-house, so seeing a job sent to an agency without the chance to work on it	Seeing a project you worked really hard on being produced and used in the real world, and hearing that it's well-received for its purpose
Emotional attachment to a project	The variety of challenges
Clients who think of you as production instead of design	Watching ideas develop from sketch to screen
Opinions	Being creative for a living
Having to sell your work, and by extension yourself, constantly	Getting to fuck around with Illustrator, Photoshop, etc. Taking things apart, putting them back together
Being surrounded by bullshit mythology / morals / stories about design that somehow pass as wisdom	
	Making something from nothing
Pointless meetings	Solving problems
Doing what you want	Doing what you want
Subjectivity	Communication
I began my path as an artist, and art – which I would equate with creativity – is my primary form of self-expression. So the hardest part of design for me is channeling my creativity to express an external message rather than an internal one	The culture; the field attracts people from widely varied backgrounds who all share a passion for communication and creativity. Combined, these attributes contribute to an environment of fun, learning and growth

Worst	Best
Rejection	The ability to create
Design is becoming a tool of consumerism and commerce rather than culture	Seeing your designs become real
Fear of not being able to deliver an amazing solution to the client	The ability to participate in a community of intelligent and creative thinkers
Difficult clients, low pay	I enjoy going to work, I feel creatively fulfilled, my hobby is my career
Convincing clients of the real value of good design for their business	We are born with an innate sense of wonder, honed by practice to – every once in a while – pull off something grand
Pressure to do great work	Potential to do great work
Getting a glimpse into different businesses	Making the complex simple
Non-creatives think what we do just 'happens' and don't realize the thought and care put into things. Most seem to think 'it's all just Photoshop'	Being able to create and impact upon the world by making it a more beautiful place
Comic Sans	Underconsideration.com
Self-doubt	The possibilities are endless
Feedback	Learning about different subjects
Chasing down payments	Getting to interpret content and ideas through form for a living, thereby helping people communicate in ways they could not have conceived on their own
We are too critical. We are too often obsessed with details, at the expense of the bigger picture	The ability to see beauty in everything. Our job is to be creative

Worst	Best
Others' perception that it's easy and anybody can do it	Being creative and the process of design
Not being valued for the design work, and people thinking it's just drawing – things that anyone can do	Solving client problems through visual design
The field can sometimes be over-saturated in some areas	The opportunity to be creative and create beautiful design
There is generally not enough time or money to explore and subsequently execute projects to the caliber they deserve	The medium applies to, and can contain, any and all subjects
People underestimate you	You provide new cultural material
Having to constantly educate everyone, every time, about what you actually do and know	When a plan comes together
Watching challenging ideas get cast aside in favor of safer options or those that mimic success	I work mostly in music, and for me it's the chance to make sure great music is given the professional and compelling presentation it deserves
The pay and the disrespect	We get to design for a living
Work versus pay	Extracurriculars with co-workers
Subjectivity	Solving problems
Being unemployed	
It's very hard to shop – I'm critiquing everything!	Fun co-workers
Executives who think they are design experts when they are actually design incompetents	Occasionally, I get to work on some interesting projects
Dealing with clients who know how to 'design'	Creating something unique and strategically sound from scratch

Worst	Best
All the badly kerned type you see all around you every day	Doing what you love for a living
'Can you make the logo bigger?'	Saying 'no' to that question
Not having enough time for family and friends	Extremely rewarding and changing challenges
Trying to know all the names of things	Expression
Compromising with people who don't know any better	Making something out of nothing
Dealing with non-designers	The creative opportunities
The ease with which your discipline can be applied to empty and potentially harmful things	The ease with which design can represent any topic or concept
Clients	Making the world look better
Having your thoughts and ideas trounced by people who can't / don't understand them	Making things, and being surrounded by a creative atmosphere
Being creative within a timeline	The ability to spread a visual idea so far out into the world
Horrible clients	Getting paid to solve problems visually
Specifically in relation to print and graphics, it seems like opportunity for growth is limited. This is why I'm moving more towards the digital space and UX design	Enjoying making creative solutions that have benefits and are used in the real world
Having little time to innovate is stifling	The requirement for innovation is refreshing
Explaining what it is	Designing

Worst	Best
Most people don't really understand what you do	Making things
Clients	Freedom
People who are not designers not taking it seriously	Working from home and making my own agenda
Bad clients	Creating
Bad feedback	Seeing the final thing
Working with committees and / or non-creatively trained people	Creating the intangible
Deadlines	Getting to know new topics / subjects / themes / people / cultures
Creative blocks	Getting paid to do something fun
Time constraints	Getting to be creative and curious about so many different subjects
Clients	Clients
	Working with type and art together
Client management	Organising your own time
Friends asking for favors	Being able to create stuff
Other people	Other people
Stupid people	The diversity of subjects you deal with

Life

This section explores that much-used term 'work-life balance'. While this was a survey of professional life, social scientists are also interested in what respondents' personal and family life can reveal, and how personal and professional worlds intersect.

It seems that designers are a reasonably social bunch, with 30% meeting up socially with friends or family several times or more a week. We're not sure whether the 1% who reported never socialising are chained to their desks, but it was definitely the case that the self-professed obsessives [see p262] spent less time meeting up socially.

Although most designers had never taken time out of their working careers, those who had taken a career break had done so for a range of reasons. We were interested to find that some respondents took the time out to re-evaluate, retrain and recover from 'burnout' [see p412].

The majority [61%] of respondents were married or cohabiting with a partner, and in general, designers' partners earned more and worked shorter hours than them. This made us wonder how many designers' home and financial lives are supported by their partners' choices... and led us to conclude that there must be other upsides to dating a designer!

How often do you meet socially with friends, relatives or work colleagues?

15%

less than once a month

Respondents who were not obsessed by their subject were more likely to socialise once a week or more.

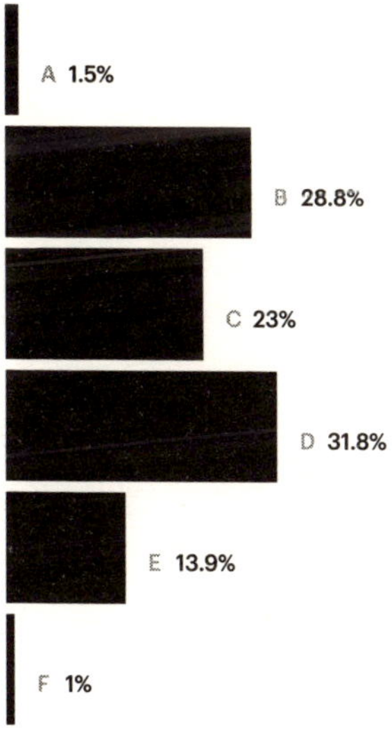

= 1,215 people

A Every day
B Several times a week
C Once a week
D Several times a month
E Less than once a month
F Never

Are you married or cohabiting with a partner?

61%

married or cohabiting

406–407

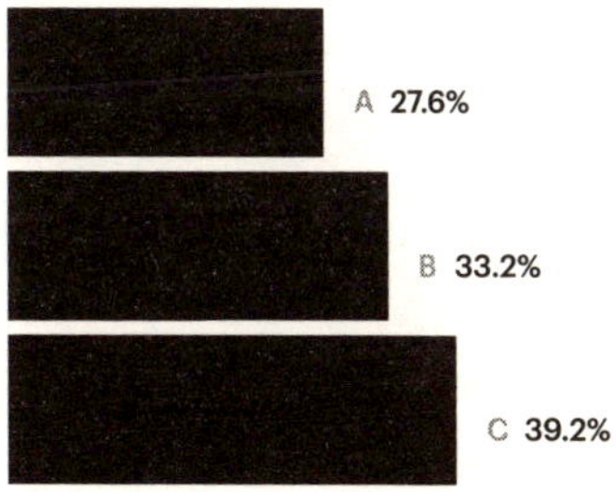

= 1,211 people

A Married
B Cohabiting with partner
C Not married, not cohabiting

What is your partner's annual income before tax?

On average, respondents earned less than their partners.

= 650 people

How many hours does he / she normally work a week?

408–409

On average, respondents worked longer hours than their partners.

= 677 people

Life

Have you ever taken time out of your working career?

NO

47.6% of those who took time out did so when aged 26–34.

YES

=
1,226
people

3pt
=
1%

71.4% No
28.6% Yes

Life: took time out of working career

For what reason?

Caring for an elderly / ill person	1.7%
Education / training	21.8%
Parental leave	16%
Personal illness or injury	10%
Voluntary time out	32.1%
Other	18.3%

Among 'other' reasons given for taking time out were travelling, re-evaluating career path and burnout.

=
349
people

Opinions

We know that graphic designers have opinions. So, alongside the standard social science questions we took the opportunity to ask about things that interested us, or that are often asked in the design industry.

We found that respondents were politically engaged: they were more likely to vote than the average citizen in the UK or US – and once at the ballot box tended to vote for left-leaning parties. But they sometimes have to compromise their principles: only 20% had never felt compromised ethically in their work and a lot more respondents disagree with free pitching than could say they never do it.

Designers were conclusive about the future of print: it's not dying any time soon, and they would definitely prefer to have their work in a book than on a blog. On other questions, they weren't so sure: for example, the respondents were split on whether graphic design is becoming a young person's profession. And we now know better than to ask for favourite Pantone colours – or at least to make allowances for those who 'think in hex' or prefer cmyk, or who just don't have a swatch book to hand!

Did you vote in the last national election?

70%

yes

Of UK respondents, 68.4% voted.
Of US respondents, 73.1% voted.

As well as being more politically active than their UK counterparts, US designers are significantly more active than their compatriots.

= 1,969 people

█ = 1 person

In the 2010 UK general election, voter turnout was 65.1%. [1]

In the 2012 US presidential election, voter turnout was 58.7%. [2]

Opinions: UK voters

What party did you vote for?

Labour	35%
Liberal Democrats	35%
Conservative	12.7%
Green	12.5%
Other	4.8%

GD& wonders...
How designers had voted in the 2015 UK election!

= 763 people

Results of the 2010 UK general election: [3]

29%	Labour
23%	Liberal Democrats
36.1%	Conservative
1%	Green
11%	Other

Opinions: US voters

What party did you vote for?

Democratic	77.3%
Republican	11.5%
Libertarian	3.8%
Green	3.8%
Other	3.6%

In general, respondents showed more left-leaning voting patterns than their national averages. Those who voted outside the UK and the US showed similar preferences.

= 419 people

Results of the 2012 US presidential election: [4]

51%	Democratic
47.2%	Republican
1%	Libertarian
0.4%	Green
0.4%	Other

Opinions

Do you adhere to a particular set of design principles in your practice?

72%

yes

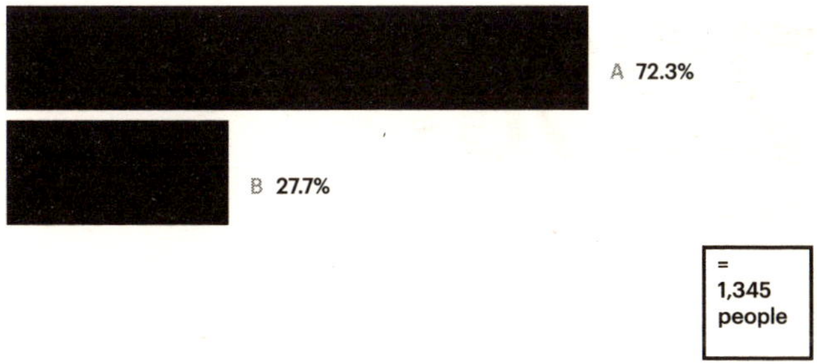

A Yes
B No

Opinions

On the whole, would your clients understand what 'adhering to design principles' means?

28%

yes

GD& wonders...
Does this help explain designer / client friction?

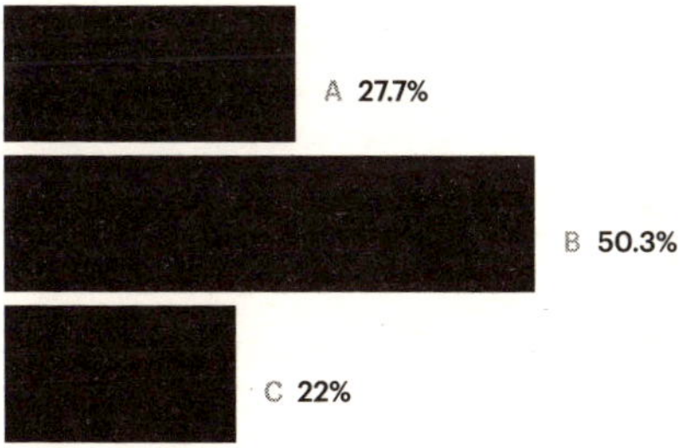

= 1,338 people

A Yes
B No
C Don't know

Opinions

Which term best describes your design approach?

31.5% user-

13.2% minimalist

9.2% modernist

5.1% experimental

1.2% expressionist

1.1% ethical

0.7% activist

centred

24.6%
conceptual

4.3% socially responsive

2% classicist

1.8% postmodernist

=
1,323
people

2pt
=
1%

31.5%	User-centred
24.6%	Conceptual
13.2%	Minimalist
9.2%	Modernist
5.3%	Other
5.1%	Experimental
4.3%	Socially responsive
2%	Classicist
1.8%	Postmodernist
1.2%	Expressionist
1.1%	Ethical
0.7%	Activist

Opinions

Do you ever feel compromised ethically in your work?

20%

never felt compromised ethically in their work

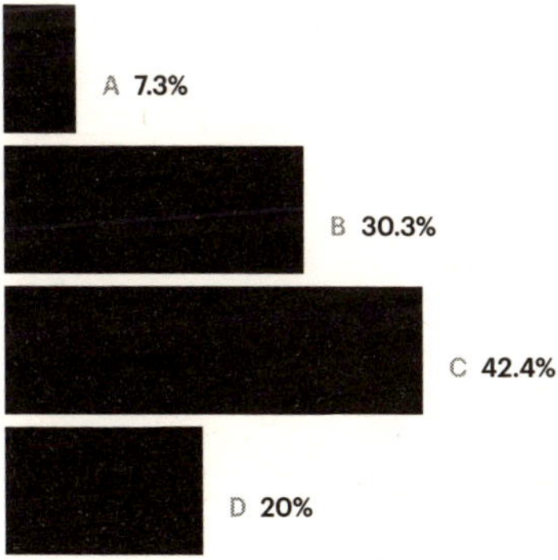

= 1,346 people

A Often
B Sometimes
C Rarely
D Never

Opinions

Do you do free pitching? Do you agree with free pitching?

60%

gave the same answer to both questions

This matrix shows the relationship between the answers given to these two questions. The denser the black, the more respondents gave that particular combination of answers.

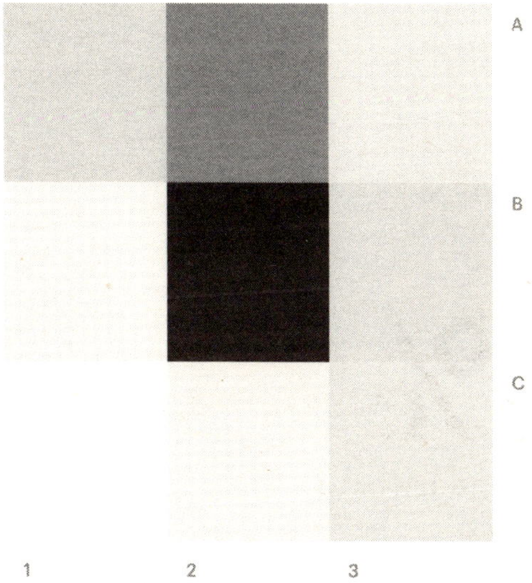

Do you do free pitching?
A **Yes**
B **No**
C **Don't know**

Do you agree with free pitching?
1 **Yes**
2 **No**
3 **Don't know**

= **1,345 people**

Opinions

Do you think graphic design is becoming more of a young person's profession?

Yes	39.5%
No	38.7%
Don't know	21.7%

= 1,348 people

Opinions

Do you think graphic design is becoming more of a young person's profession?

Total

60+

50s

40s

30s

20s

<20

A	B	C	D
■ 39.5%	■ 35.7%	■ 46.6%	■ 40.1%
■ 38.8%	■ 50%	■ 34.5%	■ 39.5%
■ 21.7%	■ 14.3%	■ 19%	■ 20.4%
= 1,348 people	= 14 people	= 58 people	= 152 people

E	F	G	
■ 29.3%	■ 43.4%	■ 52%	■ Yes
■ 49.7%	■ 34.3%	■ 16%	■ No
■ 21%	■ 22.3%	■ 32%	■ Don't know

= 352 people	= 740 people	= 25 people

Opinions

What do you think most advantages a graphic designer in the advancement of their career?

40.4% hard

28.3% who

17.8% talent

1.4% which college they went to

1.3% family background in related areas

work

they know

5.7% what they know

5.1% client list

= 1,345 people

2pt = 1%

40.4%	Hard work
28.3%	Who they know
17.8%	Talent
5.7%	What they know
5.1%	Client list
1.4%	Which college they went to
1.3%	Family background in related areas

Opinions

In 10 years' time, do you imagine that:

69.7% **print is**

29.5% print is a rarefied niche activity

still alive and well

0.8%

= 1,347 people

69.7%	Print is still alive and well
29.5%	Print is a rarefied niche activity
0.8%	Print is dead

1pt = 1%

Opinions

Would you consider it a greater success to have your work featured on a high-profile blog or in a book?

66.7% **book**

33.3% **blog**

=
1,330
people

1.5pt
=
1%

Opinions

What is your favourite Pantone colour?

Favourite Pantone colour visualisations

Stefanie Posavec, data designer

This question was meant to be a bit light-hearted, so it was quite funny to see how many slightly grumpy, sarcastic responses we received in reply. I knew I had to highlight this wayward streak in designers [I'll include myself in this statement] and also to explore the Pantone responses in more detail as a thank you to the 77% who answered the question in good faith.

As well as identifying favourite individual Pantone colours, I also went through and grouped the responses into 'types' of colour. This allowed me to look more closely at which colours were popular – and with who. Monochrome shades and metallics were particularly popular with men, while greens, pinks and fluorescents were more likely to be chosen by women.

Opinions

Favourite Pantone colour: cheeky

8%

responded sarcastically or cheekily

=
888
people

As the graph of sarcastic responses by gender shows, the majority of these respondents were men.

444-445

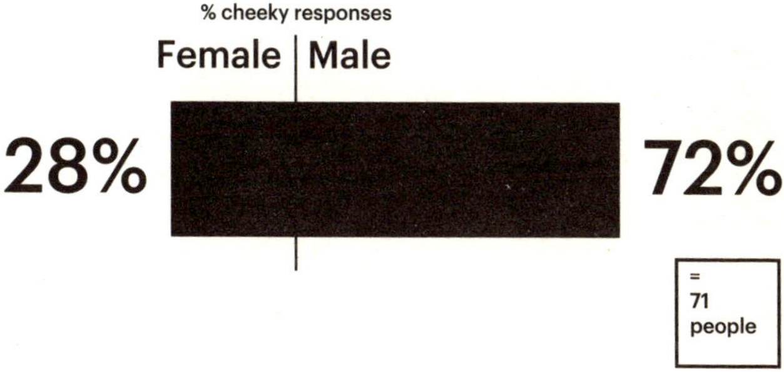

Opinions
Favourite Pantone colour:
selected responses

Is this a joke?

‘Favourite’ is the kind of concept a bad client has

Don’t be ridiculous

Knowing the PMS number of your favorite color is a ridiculous affectation

Don’t be so nerdy!

Designers shouldn’t have favorite colors

n/a – I’m not a design wanker

Survey descends into self-parody

This question is bland and I cannot be bothered to pick up my swatch book to find the exact beige

Opinions

Favourite Pantone colour: rainbow

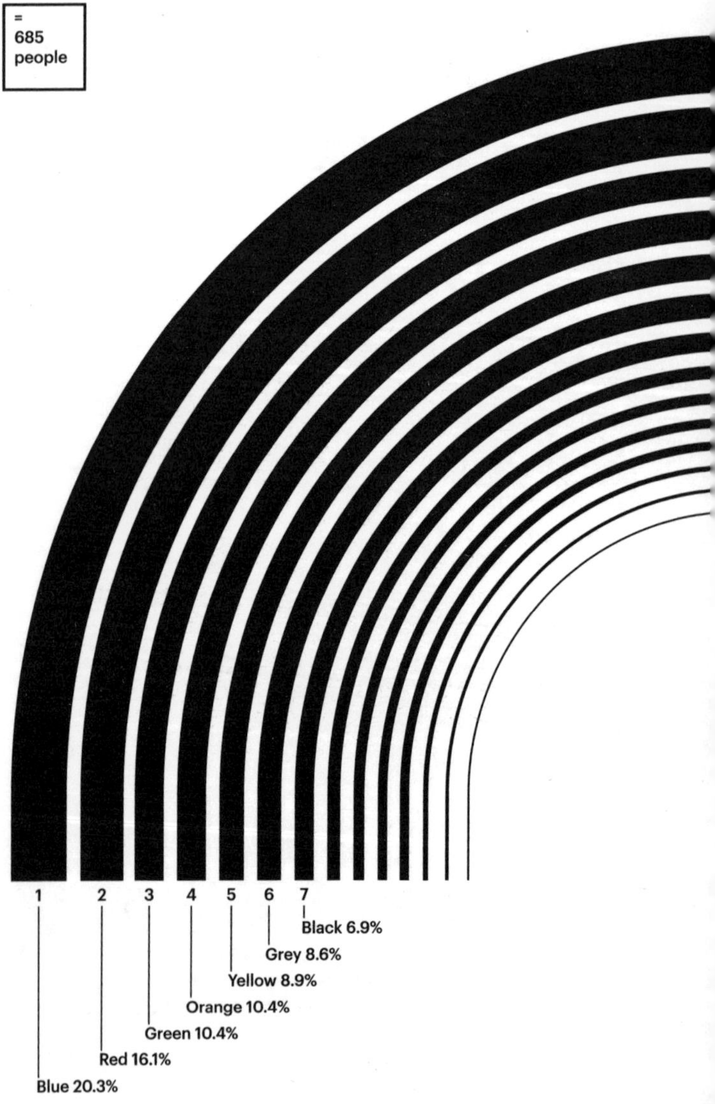

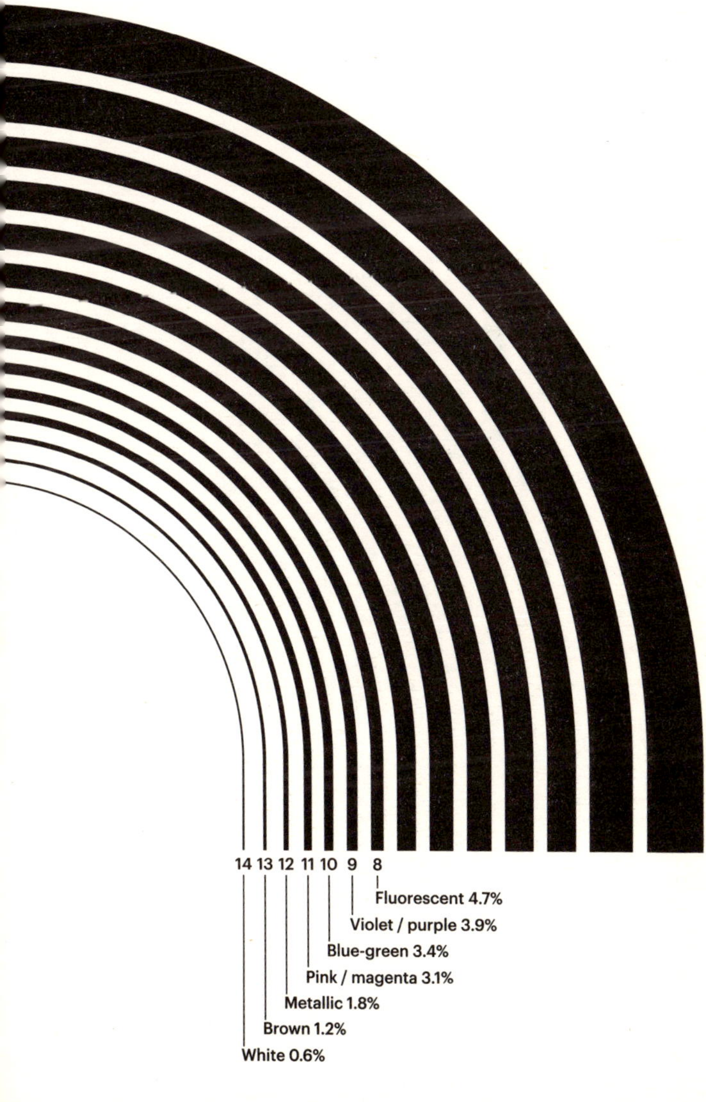

14 13 12 11 10 9 8
Fluorescent 4.7%
Violet / purple 3.9%
Blue-green 3.4%
Pink / magenta 3.1%
Metallic 1.8%
Brown 1.2%
White 0.6%

Opinions

Favourite Pantone colour: gender bias

Higher percentage of women

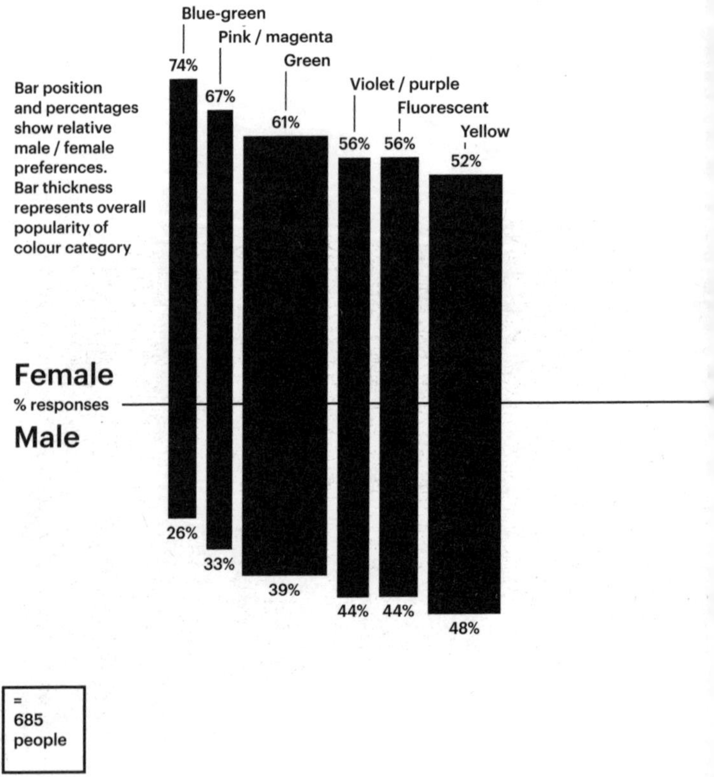

Higher percentage of men

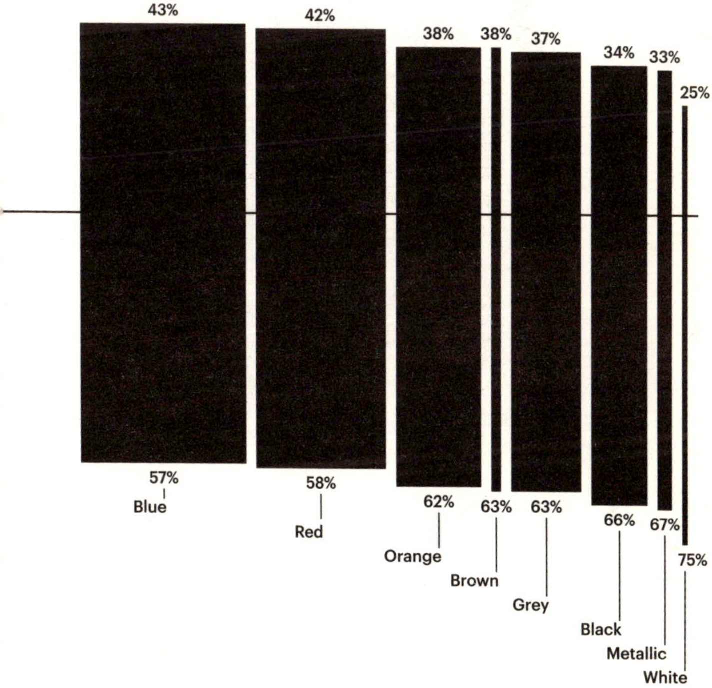

Opinions

Top five favourite Pantone colours*

Rank	Pantone	% of all respondents
1	Pantone Orange 021	3.3%
	Orange**	
2	Pantone Black	2.8%
	Black	
3	Pantone Red 032	2.6%
	Canadian Flag Red	
4	Pantone 805	2.3%
	Fluorescent Red	

=5 Pantone 186 1.4%

Stop Sign*** Red

=5 Pantone 485 1.4%

London Bus Red

=5 Pantone Reflex Blue 1.4%

European Union Blue

* Additional colour descriptions indicate where this Pantone number is the colour standard for this flag or object.

** For reference, see the cover of this book.

*** UK only. In the US, the stop sign Pantone standard is just one swatch over at Pantone 187.

And finally...

Although 83% of respondents said they would recommend a career in graphic design [see p264], only 55% of respondents expressed satisfaction with their career – and 23% were actively dissatisfied. Different surveys suggest a range of comparisons... a 2014 report by The Conference Board, a New York-based non-profit research group, put overall job satisfaction in the US at 48%. [1] Taking this as a benchmark, our sample group is more satisfied than the average. On the other hand, 2009–10 data from the UK suggested that 78% of workers were 'somewhat, mostly or completely satisfied' with their job. [2] Against that, our respondents are less satisfied than the norm.

Take a look at p314 for some of the factors contributing to designers' happiness [or not!] at work. Overall, designers were happier with their lives than their work, see p460.

And finally...

All things considered, how satisfied are you with your career?

55%

satisfied

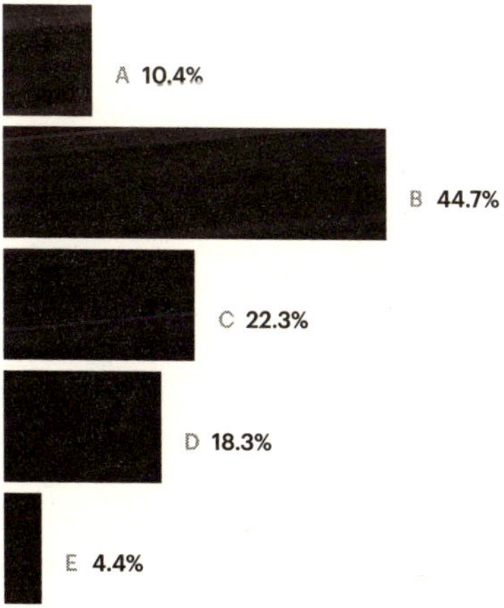

= 1,333 people

In 2014, graphic design ranked 184 out of 274 occupations in a UK Cabinet Office report on life satisfaction. [3]

A Very satisfied
B Fairly satisfied
C Neutral
D Fairly unsatisfied
E Very unsatisfied

And finally...

All things considered, how satisfied are you with your life?

67%

satisfied

36.2% of respondents were more satisfied with their life than their careers.

460–461

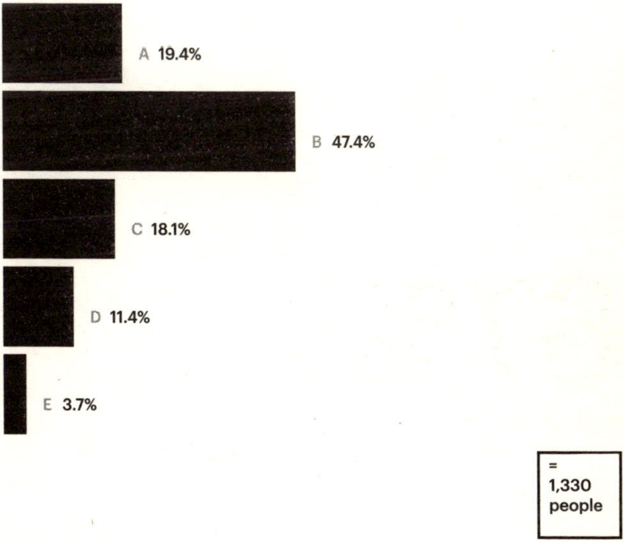

A Very satisfied
B Fairly satisfied
C Neutral
D Fairly unsatisfied
E Very unsatisfied

Survey

The survey was designed to take respondents through different routes depending on their answers. The numbering of the secondary questions reflects the order in which respondents would have answered them.

462-463

Survey

Primary questions

Do you work, study or practise in the UK or US?

1 Tell us a bit about you

Are you female or male?

How old are you?

What citizenship do you hold?

What is your annual income before tax?

What is your ethnic group?

Did you vote in the last national election?

2 Your education

What is the highest level of education you have successfully completed?

What level did you study the following art and design subjects to?

Graphic design
Illustration
Fine art
Other art and design

Did you study something other than / as well as an art and design subject at degree level or higher?

3 Your work

Which of the following best describe your specialisms? Choose all that apply:

Advertising
Animation
Art direction
Branding
Editorial design
Film-making
Graphic design
Illustration
Information design
Interaction design
Moving image
Programming
Type design
Typography
Web design
Other [please specify]

Which of the following best describes your primary specialism:

Advertising
Animation
Art direction
Branding
Editorial design
Film-making
Graphic design
Illustration
Information design
Interaction design
Moving image
Programming
Type design
Typography
Web design
Other [please specify]

Which of the following best describes your current occupation? Choose all that apply:

Paid a salary or wage by an employer
Managing a business
Partner in a business
Running own business
Doing freelance work
Student
Educator / academic
Intern
Unemployed / not in work
Retired

4 The way you work

Do you adhere to a particular set of design principles in your practice?

On the whole, would your clients understand what this means?

Which term best describes your design approach:

Activist
Classicist
Conceptual
Ethical
Experimental
Expressionist
Minimalist
Modernist
Postmodernist
Socially responsive
User-centred
Other [please specify]

As a practising designer, have you been strategic in targeting particular types of work?

If yes, do you think this strategy has been successful?

In a given year, what percentage of your work needs to consist of creatively fulfilling projects for you to feel content?

Do you work more hours than you are paid to work?

Have you, or the company you work for, ever said 'no' to a job?

If yes, was the main reason related to:

Creative limitations
Ethical considerations
Financial considerations
Time limitations
Poor client relationship

Do you ever feel compromised ethically in your work?

Do you do free pitching / speculative work?

Do you agree with free pitching / speculative work?

Are you designing what you thought you would be designing when you started your career?

In a typical working day, approximately how much of your time do you spend designing?

What are you doing at work when you are not designing? Choose the three most frequent activities:

Answering emails
Budgeting / scheduling
Commissioning
Going to meetings
Keeping up with contemporary art and design [gallery visits, exhibitions, reading, etc]
PR / communications
Project-related research
Sourcing / liaising with suppliers
Writing tenders / bids / requests for proposals

Do you work directly with coders / programmers?

Can you code / program?

Have you done any teaching in your subject?

If yes, at what level?

If yes, please specify how you worked. Choose all that apply:

Fixed term contract
Guest lecturing
Permanent contract
Regular hourly paid

What skill do you think it would be most useful for you to develop or acquire?

Art direction
Budgeting
Idea generation
Image making
Knowledge of the field
Moving image
Networking
Preparing work for print
Presentation skills
Proficiency at Adobe CS
Programming / coding
Project management
Research
Self-promotion
Strategy
Time management
Typography
Writing
Other [please specify]

In the past year, approximately what percentage of your work was for the following sectors?

Charities and NGOs
Cultural
Government
Private business
Pro bono
Self-initiated

What proportion of your commercial work is commissioned by clients?

5 Promoting your work

Generally speaking, how do you get work?

Generally speaking, how comfortable do you feel promoting your work?

Have you ever spoken publicly about your work [eg giving a lecture, speaking at a conference]?

How often would you say you:

Seek out projects / clients / opportunities?
Attend networking events?
Volunteer to speak about your work?

Generally, how quickly do you follow up on new contacts?

Has anyone ever nominated your or your studio's work for an award or competition?

Have you or your studio ever entered work for an award or competition?

If yes, how often over the course of your career?

Have you or your studio ever won an award or competition?

Have you ever been a judge for an award or competition?

6 Part-time / full-time work

Do you work part- or full-time in your main job?

Do you work part- or full-time overall [even if your work comprises various part-time jobs]?

7 Your time at work

In the past week, were you working predominantly as an employee or were you self-employed / running your own business?

How many people are employed in your main place of work?

How long have you been working within design, in years?

Generally, how many hours do you work in a week?

Would you prefer to work more or fewer hours than you presently work?

Do you ever get bored by your work?

Are you a member of a trade union or staff association?

Are any of the people at your place of work members of a trade union or staff association?

Please list any professional organisations you are a member of.

Have you ever taken time out of your working career?

If yes, at what age?

And for what reason:

Personal illness or injury
Parental leave
Caring for an elderly or ill relative / friend
Education / training
Voluntary time out
Other [please specify]

8 Your time outside work

How often do you meet socially with friends, relatives or work colleagues?

Are you married or cohabiting with a partner?

9 Do you have young children?

Do you or your partner have children under eight years of age?

10 Money and housing

Which of the following best describes how you feel about your / your family's present income?

Living very comfortably
Living comfortably
Getting by
Finding it difficult
Finding it very difficult

Which of the following best describes how you feel about your / your family's financial security?

Income is predictable and secure
Income is unpredictable and I feel ok about this
Income is unpredictable and I find this difficult

Do you have a pension / retirement account?

Do you have income protection / insurance against loss of earnings due to sickness?

Do you have private health cover / insurance?

Which of the following best describes your housing situation:

Living rent-free with family
Living rent-free with friends / others
Renting on my own
Renting with friends / others
Renting with a partner and / or children
Own by myself
Own with friends / others
Own with a partner

Do you have a mortgage?

Do you have a second property?

Are you a landlord?

11 Lastly, your opinions on...

Do you think graphic design is becoming more of a young person's profession?

Do you think that the graphic design industry is:

A feminine culture
A masculine culture
A gender-neutral culture
Don't know

In 10 years' time, do you imagine that:

Print is dead
Print is a rarefied niche activity
Print is still alive and well

Do you think you have to be able to withstand rejection to be successful?

Have you generally found negative feedback on your work to be:

An interesting challenge
Constructive
Dispiriting
Humiliating
Infuriating
Irrelevant
Motivating
Not an issue

Have your work-related role models primarily been:

Graphic designers
Not graphic designers
I don't have any work-related role models

Would you say that you are obsessed with your subject?

Do you think it would be a positive thing if clients attended design conferences?

How do you think your most recent work compares to that of your peers?

All things considered, how satisfied are you with:

Your career
Your life

What do you think most advantages a graphic designer in the advancement of their career:

Hard work
Client list
Talent
Family background in related areas
Which college they went to
What they know
Who they know

Would you consider it a greater success to have your work featured on a high-profile blog or in a book?

Do you keep an archive in the hope of that future retrospective?

What is your favourite Pantone colour?

What is the worst thing about being a designer?

What is the best thing about being a designer?

Would you recommend graphic design as a career choice?

Secondary questions

1.1 You voted in the UK

What party did you vote for:

Conservative
Green
Labour
Liberal Democrats
Plaid Cymru
Scottish National
UK Independence
Other [please specify]

1.1 You voted outside the UK

Please choose the option which best describes the party you voted for:

Centre-left
Centre-right
Conservative
Nationalist
Socialist
Social democrat
Other [please specify]

1.1 You voted in the US

What party did you vote for:

Democratic
Green
Libertarian
Republican
Other [please specify]

1.1 You voted outside the US

Please choose the option which best describes the party you voted for:

Centre-left
Centre-right
Conservative
Nationalist
Socialist
Social democrat
Other [please specify]

2.1 You studied something other than / as well as an art and design subject at degree level or higher

In what field was this:

Engineering / technology
Humanities
Mathematics
Natural sciences
Social sciences
Other [please specify]

3.1 You run your own business

Is your business registered as a limited company / corporation?

How many people work in your business?

What word would you use to describe your business:

Agency
Atelier
Collective
Company
Foundry
Partnership
Practice
Studio
Workshop

Do you have interns?

If yes, are they:

Paid a wage or salary
Paid expenses
Unpaid
A mix of paid and unpaid

Do you know the legal rights of interns?

3.1 You are an intern

Are you paid:

Nothing
Expenses
A wage / salary

How many internships have you done?

On average, how long do they last?

Have any of your internships led to contracted employment?

How long do you expect to be an intern for?

How important do you think internships are in achieving employment in graphic design?

What was your main motivation to become an intern:

Developing a network
Gaining knowledge of different studios
Gaining professional experience
Improving skills
It's a direct route to employment
Lack of full employment opportunities

How did you get your current internship:

Advertisement
Direct approach from studio
Links from course / college
Recommendation
Self-initiated
Direct approach
Word of mouth
Other

Do you know the legal rights of interns?

3.1 You are a student

What are you studying:

Communication design / visual communication
Graphic design
Illustration
Other [please specify]

At what level?

Are you the first person in your family to go on to higher education?

Do you want to become a practising professional in your field of study when you finish your degree?

Do you think you will become a practising professional in your field of study when you finish your degree?

How do you hope to be employed when you enter the profession?

Paid a salary or wage by an employer
Managing a business
Partner in a business
Running your own business
Doing freelance work
Educator / academic

What skill do you think it would be most useful for you to develop or acquire:

Art direction
Budgeting
Idea generation
Image making
Knowledge of the field
Moving image
Networking
Preparing work for print
Presentation skills
Proficiency at Adobe CS
Programming / coding
Project management
Research
Self-promotion
Strategy
Time management
Typography
Writing
Other [please specify]

3.1 You are an educator

What was your main motivation for becoming an educator:

To influence / challenge industry
To influence / shape the future of the discipline
To keep challenging and developing myself / my practice
To provide financial security
To pursue a research-orientated career
To teach students / share knowledge

What level do you teach at?

In your current job, what is your primary role:

Academic / scholar
Course leader
Head of department
Researcher
Senior manager
Teacher

Are you:

Hourly paid / sessional
Fixed term
Permanent / part-time
Permanent / full-time

What is the subject discipline you are teaching / leading / managing:

Communication design / visual communication
Graphic design
Illustration
Other [please specify]

Do you maintain a practice in graphic design or an associated field in addition to your role as an educator?

3.2 You maintain a practice in addition to your role as an educator

Is this as:

A freelancer
Part of a studio
Other

Is your practice mainly:

Curating
Graphic design
Illustration
Publishing
Research
Writing / commentary
Other

4.1 Your clients

In the past year, approximately what percentage of your work has been for foreign-based clients?

Of your work for foreign-based clients, approximately what percentage has been for companies based in:

Africa
Asia
Australia
Europe
North America
South America

How regularly do you meet your clients face-to-face?

How often do your clients take an active role in the design process?

How do you feel about clients taking an active role in the design process?

In your experience, is it true that your work is only 'as good as your client will let it be'?

Generally, what do you think has the biggest impact on whether clients affect the quality of your work:

Specific individuals
The sector they represent
Don't know

Have you ever been asked to 'make it bigger'?

6.1 Overall, you work part-time

Why do you work part-time:

You are also a student
You are ill or have a disability
You can't find a full-time job
You don't want a full-time job
You are looking after children
You are looking after an incapacitated adult

6.2 You are looking after children or an incapacitated adult

Are you looking after children / an incapacitated adult because:

Suitable care services are not available
Suitable care services are not affordable
You have chosen to be a carer

7.1 You took parental leave

How long did you take?

And was your parental leave:

A legal entitlement
Allowed by your employer [contractual parental leave]
Voluntary leave
A combination of legal / contractual leave and voluntary leave
Don't know

Was your job secure over the course of your parental leave?

Did your partner / spouse take parental leave?

8.1 You are married or cohabiting with a partner

What does your partner / spouse do?

Is your partner / spouse:

Paid a salary or wage by an employer
Running a business
A partner in a business
Working for her / himself
Doing freelance work
A student
An educator / academic
A paid intern
An unpaid intern
Unemployed / not in work
Retired

How many hours does he / she normally work per week?

What is her / his annual income before tax?

What is the highest level of education s/he has completed?

9.1 About your young children

How old is your youngest child?

Who is primarily responsible for your child's / children's day-to-day care?

Are you / have you been entitled to free or subsidised childcare paid for by your employer?

If you share childcare responsibilities with a partner / spouse, how satisfied are you with the way childcare tasks are divided?

Sources*

You

[1] **Design Council:**
***Design Industry Research*, 2010**
bit.ly/1VZ4KFJ
[2] **Office for National Statistics**
bit.ly/1qMfFRI
[3] **US Census Bureau**
1.usa.gov/1XaHUrK
[4] **Design Council:**
***Design Industry Research*, 2010**
bit.ly/1VZ4KFJ
[5] ***The Guardian***
bit.ly/1VJqIss
[6] **US Census Bureau**
1.usa.gov/1LUvSkt

UK / US

[1] **Gallup**
bit.ly/1tSj56s
[2] **Office for National Statistics**
bit.ly/1QDbS3I
[3] ***The Boston Globe***
bit.ly/1mMBlYx
[4] **Office for National Statistics**
bit.ly/1OKJwWj
[5] **US Census Bureau**
1.usa.gov/KWEGYk
[6] **Office for National Statistics**
bit.ly/1m3Sc9t
[7] **US Census Bureau**
1.usa.gov/1jAtEVk
[8] **Office for National Statistics**
bit.ly/1VXCMEL
[9] **US Bureau of Labor Statistics**
1.usa.gov/1RO1ib5
[10] **Office for National Statistics, 2015**
bit.ly/1hK74gS **[the second table]**
[11] **US Bureau of Labor Statistics, 2015**
1.usa.gov/1W9r3sn

Gender

[1] **UK Government consultation:**
***Closing the Gender Pay Gap*, 2015**
bit.ly/1LUwA1O
[2] **US Bureau of Labor Statistics, 2014**
1.usa.gov/1Gk4oBy
[3] **Design Museum, London**
bit.ly/1GaYzY2
[4] **Fatherhood Institute**
bit.ly/1KfHN4R

Education

[1] **Design Council:**
***Design Industry Research*, 2010**
bit.ly/1VZ4KFJ
[2] **Ibid.**
[3] ***The Washington Post***
wapo.st/1LfY5yE
[4] **Design Council:**
***Design Industry Research*, 2010**
bit.ly/1VZ4KFJ
[5] ***The Guardian* / Higher Education Statistics Agency**
bit.ly/1Hg9qei

Work

[1] US Bureau of Labor statistics: *Occupational Outlook Handbook [Graphic Design]*, 2012
1.usa.gov/1GaYu6P

[2] Design Council: *Design Industry Research*, 2010
bit.ly/1VZ4KFJ

[3] Office for National Statistics
bit.ly/1PyfTrl

[4] Department for Business, Innovation & Skills
bit.ly/1LUfWbI

[5] US Small Business Administration
1.usa.gov/19cinHw

[6] European Commission
bit.ly/1wQ0Yxo

[7] Department for Business Innovation & Skills
bit.ly/1RO1xD0

[8] US Bureau of Labor Statistics
1.usa.gov/KlnM6w

[9] UK Government
bit.ly/1O282Bi

[10] US Department of Labor
1.usa.gov/1k4SYmh

[11] US Department of Labor
1.usa.gov/19SWGgf

[12] UK Government
bit.ly/1jKZPUU

[13] Design Museum, London
bit.ly/1GaYzY2

Clients

[1] Department for Culture, Media & Sport: *Creative industries: Focus on Exports*, 2015
bit.ly/1PyfZzA

Money

[1] Office for National Statistics
bit.ly/1xnGsH3

[2] Living Wage Foundation
bit.ly/1e9B1yi

[3] Office for National Statistics
bit.ly/1oyioy0

[4] US Census Bureau
1.usa.gov/1FnKZii [p5]

Opinions

[1] UK Political Info
bit.ly/1y2RqnN

[2] www.nonprofitvote.org: *America Goes to the Polls*
bit.ly/1Kflg7f

[3] BBC
bbc.in/1GaYQua

[4] Federal Election Commission
1.usa.gov/1lR3sEF

And finally...

[1] The Conference Board
bit.ly/1wz8Y3S

[2] Office for National Statistics
bit.ly/1LXhKR9

[3] BBC
bbc.in/1kOwDuf

* All links accessed 28 October 2015.

Thank you

to all our survey respondents who gave their time and shared their opinions so generously

and

our experts

Nikandre Kopcke for her tenacity, sense of fun and knowledge of the field

Stefanie Posavec for her fresh ideas and dexterity with data

our GD& associates

Jessie Price for her mathematical brain, persistence and for being there when the going gets tough

Sarah Schrauwen for her design intuition, eye for detail and many late nights

and the other members of the GD& team, without whom this book would not have been possible

Lorna Fray
Robert Hetherington
John McGill
David Shaw

and

to our families, who continue to support us in our long and compelling endeavour

Damian Wayling
Katy Roberts-Wayling
Ray Roberts

Lawrence Zeegen
Patrick Wright
Judy Wright

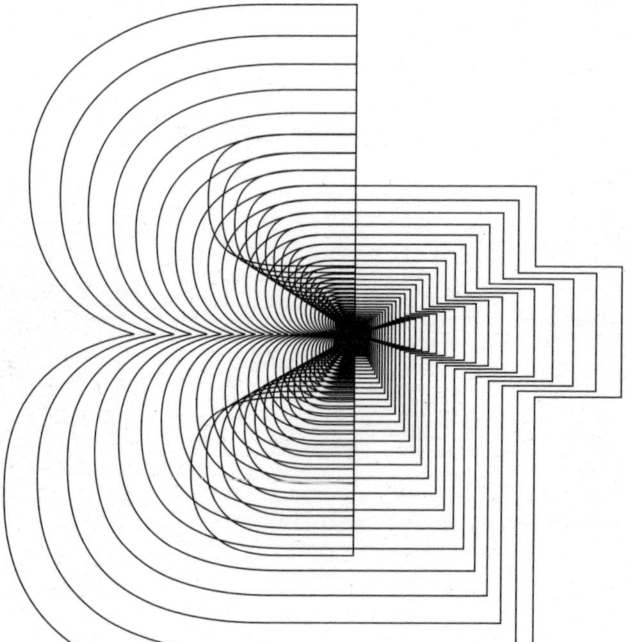